D0789360

WITHDRAWN
UTSA LIBRARIES

Innovative Lean Development

How to Create, Implement and Maintain a Learning Culture Using Fast Learning Cycles

WITHDRAWN
UTSA LIBRARIES

Innovative Lean Development

How to Create, Implement and Maintain a Learning Culture Using Fast Learning Cycles

Timothy Schipper and Mark Swets

CRC Press
Taylor & Francis Group
Boca Raton   London   New York

CRC Press is an imprint of the
Taylor & Francis Group, an **informa** business

A PRODUCTIVITY PRESS BOOK

Productivity Press
Taylor & Francis Group
270 Madison Avenue
New York, NY 10016

© 2010 by Taylor and Francis Group, LLC
Productivity Press is an imprint of Taylor & Francis Group, an Informa business

No claim to original U.S. Government works

Printed in the United States of America on acid-free paper
10 9 8 7 6 5 4 3 2 1

International Standard Book Number: 978-1-4200-9298-1 (Paperback)

This book contains information obtained from authentic and highly regarded sources. Reasonable efforts have been made to publish reliable data and information, but the author and publisher cannot assume responsibility for the validity of all materials or the consequences of their use. The authors and publishers have attempted to trace the copyright holders of all material reproduced in this publication and apologize to copyright holders if permission to publish in this form has not been obtained. If any copyright material has not been acknowledged please write and let us know so we may rectify in any future reprint.

Except as permitted under U.S. Copyright Law, no part of this book may be reprinted, reproduced, transmitted, or utilized in any form by any electronic, mechanical, or other means, now known or hereafter invented, including photocopying, microfilming, and recording, or in any information storage or retrieval system, without written permission from the publishers.

For permission to photocopy or use material electronically from this work, please access www.copyright.com (http://www.copyright.com/) or contact the Copyright Clearance Center, Inc. (CCC), 222 Rosewood Drive, Danvers, MA 01923, 978-750-8400. CCC is a not-for-profit organization that provides licenses and registration for a variety of users. For organizations that have been granted a photocopy license by the CCC, a separate system of payment has been arranged.

Trademark Notice: Product or corporate names may be trademarks or registered trademarks, and are used only for identification and explanation without intent to infringe.

Library of Congress Cataloging-in-Publication Data

Schipper, Timothy.
 Innovative lean development : how to create, implement and maintain a learning culture using fast learning cycles / Timothy Schipper and Mark Swets.
  p. cm.
 Includes bibliographical references and index.
 ISBN 978-1-4200-9298-1
 1. Lean manufacturing. 2. New products. 3. Organizational learning. 4. Organizational effectiveness. 5. Industrial management. I. Swets, Mark. II. Title.

TS155.S3135 2010
658.5--dc22   2009014518

Visit the Taylor & Francis Web site at
http://www.taylorandfrancis.com

and the Productivity Press Web site at
http://www.productivitypress.com

Library
University of Texas
at San Antonio

Dedication

This book is dedicated to our families who made it possible to set aside the time to write it and to our friends at Steelcase who helped us refine the methods described in these pages.

I dedicate the work to my loving and dedicated wife, Karen, and our children, Laura, Anna, and Peter, who supported my efforts to collect information, write, and refine the content. I am grateful for many God-given blessings, including working for a company and in a group that has allowed me to explore the concepts and principles described in this book. The process of writing about what has been accomplished over several years of effort has been complex and demanding. It is my sincere hope that the techniques that have been proven to work to improve the process of developing new solutions in our company will also work for the readers in their organizations.

Tim Schipper

I dedicate this work to my wife, Cheri, my son, John, and my daughter, Jenna. They are my constant source of joy, balance, and well-being. I am a better person because of them. Truly, I have overachieved in marriage and family. I am honored to be a part of an organization that encourages curiosity, promotes innovation, values how people work, and helps employees do what they do better. Steelcase, and Steelcase employees, are first class.

Mark Swets

Contents

Acknowledgments

We are grateful to our many friends and colleagues at Steelcase. They have willingly tried many of the new methods we describe in this work, and have been our sounding boards and provided feedback on the methods.

We are very grateful to David Mann, our mentor, who encouraged us to write this work and showed us the path to get it done. We are privileged to have a foreword written by him. David also deserves thanks for providing us with the final edits and review prior to our sending the manuscript off to the publisher.

We also appreciate the contributions of Kurt Winks, Bill Reynolds, Greg Lok, Ryan Millhouse of the Deta!ls group, who were some of the first people to adopt these methods in their work process. They allowed us to experiment and always fully supported the methods and techniques.

There are many in the information technology department, including Doug Minder, Nancy Faber, Jim Klaes, Anjela Gustaf, David Lang, Tom O'Brien, and Scott Steelman, who helped us apply these methods to the IT process. Additional thanks go to the development leaders who helped to refine these methods: Brad Dykstra, Josh Hoekstra, Larry Schafer, and Brad Youngs.

Our teammates on the lean team listened to and critiqued our approaches. Thanks go to Ryan Schmidt, Steve Smith, Becca Schmitz, and Jon VanSweden. They have all embraced the concepts of learning cycles and applied them to their own lean projects throughout the company.

We are also grateful to those outside the company who assisted and introduced these concepts to us. Jim Luckman brought us the concepts and ideas of the lean development process and of learning cycles, knowledge, and set-based design. Those concepts were first applied to information technology during lean workshops and then to product development. Jim also put us in contact with other companies who were applying these to their processes.

Bart Huthwaite showed us the methods of structured innovation and coached teams at Steelcase in this method. He also encouraged us to write this work to show others how lean and innovation go hand-in-hand. He taught us many things through his writings, workshops, and onsite coaching. Ultimately, Bart reviewed and edited our work, and we are honored to have his foreword.

Many thanks go to Maura May, publisher, and the rest of the staff of Productivity Press, who guided us through the writing and refinement of the book. Their expertise allowed us to tackle this project and move it from thoughts on the page to an integrated whole.

Foreword

by Bart Huthwaite, Sr.

Anybody can learn how to ride a bicycle, but nobody knows how we are able to do it. Not even bicycle manufacturers know the formula for the correct way to counteract the tendency to fall. Preventing a fall, an engineer once noted, "is accomplished by turning the handlebars so that for a given angle of unbalance the curvature of each turn is inversely proportional to the square of the speed at which the cyclist is moving." It is a good description. However, it does not tell us much. The bicyclist obeys principles that are known, but which he cannot specify.

Such is the case with innovation. Some project teams achieve great success, while others struggle. The winners apply principles that can be explained at the finish line, but are not clear at the start. They obey a code of rules that are specifiable, but have not been specified.

With this book, Tim Schipper and Mark Swets have made remarkable strides in not only breaking the "code of innovation" but making these principles understandable, doable, and repeatable. While innovation will always be "messy business," the authors have eliminated much of the messiness. They have brought systematic thinking to something that does not lend itself to being systematic. Innovative lean development brings substance to the quest for new, more innovative, business models.

Tim and Mark have broken with that school of thought that believes innovation, by its very nature, cannot be captured as a process. Many corporate managers still see innovation as the skill of only a few. However, almost 25 years ago, Peter Drucker, the dean of America's business and management philosophers, dismissed this notion in his bestseller *Innovation and Entrepreneurship: Practice and Principles*. Drucker flatly stated that "Innovation is capable of being presented as a discipline, capable of being learned, capable of being practiced." Drucker advised entrepreneurs to search purposefully for the sources of innovation, the changes, and their symptoms that indicate opportunities for successful innovation. "And they need to know and to apply the principles of successful innovation," he emphasized. However, Drucker made it clear that his book was not a how-to guide.

This book starts where Drucker left off. It addresses the task of how to make innovation a successful practice in a corporate environment. Heretofore, corporate environments were not known as hotbeds of innovation success. This book breaks with this notion. It shows how anyone can practice the principles of lean innovation.

I have encountered many people who can generate a lot of creative ideas. However, innovation is the task of converting these ideas into successful business models with a minimum of cost and a maximum of quality and speed. In short, innovative ideas must not only be new, they must be "lean from the start." As Tim and Mark point out, applying lean principles on the factory floor is like firefighting. Applying them at the concept stage is what is really needed—fire prevention.

As I emphasize in my book, *Rules of Innovation*, without a systematic process, innovative thinking has little chance of taking root in a company's culture. There has to be a step-by-step way to "make it happen." Such a process will not guarantee success every time, but it will increase the odds of success by a great margin.

I have encountered some people for whom innovation skills are a natural talent. Should you be one of these, it can work to your disadvantage. Your natural skill can make a job look so easy that others fail to understand how you do it. In addition, you may find it nearly impossible to teach those who want to learn from you. How can you teach what you know instinctively and never had to learn? In such cases, both you and your team members need a how-to guide in order to convert the abstraction of innovation into a step-by-step way of thinking and working. You need a way to make bicycle riding far more than natural instinct.

The intent of this book is to do just that. It is based on solid principles that can be applied again and again. With their concept of multiple learning cycles, the authors are solving one of the most perplexing problems in innovation.

A design team faces two difficulties: the first is understanding the problem; the second is finding a solution. There is no logical, straight line to success. There is no algorithm to get you there. You must continually work back and forth from problem to solution until you find the optimum choice for moving ahead.

Multiple learning cycles provide the way out of this messy problem. The problem and solution co-evolve in the same design process. Problem and solution are both developed in parallel, sometimes leading to a creative redefinition of the problem or to a solution that lies outside the boundaries of what was previously assumed to be possible.

What you need to know about the problem may only become apparent as you try to solve it. The key to design is the effective management of the dual exploration of both the problem space and the solution space.

Multiple learning cycles bring both effectiveness and efficiency to any product or service innovation challenge.

Bart Huthwaite, Sr.
Founder, Huthwaite Innovation Institute
Mackinac Island, Michigan

Foreword

by David Mann

This book is a lot like a GPS version of a treasure map. The treasure has long been rumored to be there for easy taking, but the directions on the many maps promising to lead to the treasure were problematic. Some were not specific enough to be useful. Other maps were so deep in abstruse technical detail they seemed to require an oracle to make sense of them. These maps were uninterpretable by the average person interested in actually doing lean development and too theoretical to be useful in practical application.

But now, you hold a truly useful map in your hands.

Of course, you could spend years studying Toyota, but several reporters of those efforts produced material that, again, just wasn't that helpful. Toyota is too good, too advanced, to emulate when starting from square one. Just naming a chief engineer, whatever that role actually entails, is a simple but not very effective answer. Tim and Mark were not daunted by the lack of clarity or the jargon in the lean development literature.

Nor were they held back by the lack of a workable knowledge management system, a necessary adjunct to the learning cycle approach to development. How else to preserve and retrieve what was learned in the learning cycles? Here, they took the lean sensei's classic advice in response to the question: "What can you do today?" and tackled the problem in conjunction with one of their first client lean development project teams, using hanging file folders in a milk crate to hold knowledge capture documents that were not exactly standardized, at least at the outset.

Finally, Tim and Mark took on the notion that only those with special-ized training were qualified to be innovative. They steeped themselves in the techniques of structured innovation, first to understand how it works, and then to integrate into learning cycles in lean development. This latter step has been a significant innovation in itself. It has brought these tools into regular use with all the disciplines represented on cross-functional develop-ment teams, opening eyes others had presumed to be sightless, bringing expanded possibilities and previously unimagined benefits.

Tim and Mark's book is the product of their experiences working with project teams in IT application development and teams developing new-to-the-world physical products, simple as well as complex ones. It is a work informed by concept but forged in practical application, revision, and reapplication.

I watched Tim and Mark follow their own advice. Over a period of 4 years, they treated a series of lean development projects as a sequence of learning cycles. They repeatedly adapted practice to concept, further illu-minating the concepts, and then translated them again to application and further trial. Above all, they simultaneously have been teachers as well as students. They have carefully observed practices and outcomes and then varied key elements of practice and observed again, retaining those that pro-duce a smoother process, an improved outcome.

This is truly a practitioner's book. It won't design your specific process, but it clearly lays out a path: the structure, steps, tools, and standards that, when applied, will lead you to an effective lean development process. The hard part will not be trying to divine what the authors meant, how to start, or even figuring out the length and number of learning cycles to use.

Rather, the hard part of lean development is the same as the difficult parts of any lean implementation—the human aspects of lean. These are having the courage to begin; the discipline to adhere to the process; and the confidence that even though radically different from your past practices, the process will produce results of better quality that are faster to market and less costly to develop.

Lean conversion, in any of its applications, is difficult not because of technical complexity. The difficulty comes from how very different a lean approach is from a conventional approach. The problem lies in engaging in new behaviors and practices that are contrary to those developed over time, over a career, and which have become habits.

Engaging in lean development means overcoming the habits from past practices, a serious hurdle to surmount. Tim and Mark provide practical information that helps to develop the new habits and practices that sustain a lean development project, process, and initiative.

You will find here a set of four standards for lean development, a small set but with great leverage. These are standards for the behaviors, practices, and attributes of lean development—the appropriate use of learning cycles, visual controls for development projects, application of structured innovation, and knowledge capture. If you follow the standards, you'll be putting lean development in place, and more important, you'll be ensuring the behaviors and practices that sustain it. Perhaps best of all, there is little mystery involved; these are things you can teach, expect, observe, and audit.

Do so, and you'll be pleased with the results.

David Mann
Steelcase Inc., Retired
Principal, David Mann Lean Consulting
East Grand Rapids, Michigan

Introduction

Innovation is the engine that drives industry, academia, medical discoveries, scientific research, and much of what is called success in business. Innovation has recently become a buzzword of executives, and even commercials have picked up on it to describe the products and services of various companies, including IBM, Netflix, Apple, and others. Innovation. It is a key driver. It is ubiquitous.

Innovative lean development is not a fad. It is an essential tool that incorporates the fundamental principles of lean manufacturing and the rules and behaviors of structured innovation into the development process. The marriage of the two—lean development and standard innovation—helps unleash the creativity of everyone involved in developing new products, services, or processes; speeds the process; and leads to higher quality. The authors have seen development teams apply these principles and cut their development time in half and increase their speed to market, while delivering award-winning, high-quality solutions.

While much has been written about both lean development and structured innovation methods, the idea of integrating the two has received scant attention in practice and in the literature. We hope that this book will help you and your organization become better innovative lean developers.

What Innovative Lean Development Will Do for Your Company

Over the course of time, the methods and practices of innovative lean development have been refined (and continue to be improved), and key principles have evolved that are applicable to a wide range of development projects. In this book, we explain those principles and examine how they can be used to transform your company's approach to development. We also suggest a framework you can follow to implement innovative lean development successfully.

In addition to product and information technology (IT) development, the principles of innovative lean development can be applied to the design and implementation of new services.

Marketer and designer, analyst and programmer, and business planner and program developer can all benefit from the application of fast learning cycles, or short, focused development bursts, which dramatically reduce the amount of rework in any development project and speed up the development process.

Implementing Innovative Lean Development

The authors' lean manufacturing history goes back to the 1980s when in our company, as in many organizations, quality programs and continuous improvement projects, known as World Class Manufacturing (WCM), were first used to improve the manufacturing infrastructure. Around 1996, the company switched its focus from WCM to lean manufacturing solutions. In 2001, economic conditions were forcing our customers to delay capital spending.

In 2003, the company expanded its lean efforts beyond manufacturing and implemented lean principles across the entire enterprise. The first efforts applied the principles to typical transactional processes in the office, including product catalog production, accounting, and order management. The effort started slowly but quickly gained momentum as successes mounted. In 2005, the first teams started experimenting with applying lean principles to development, specifically to IT development projects, with a great deal of success.

One of the earliest successes came from the team that implemented SAP (from the German, Systeme, Anwendungen und Produkte in der Datenverarbeitung, literally translated as "Systems, Applications and Products in Data Processing") manufacturing applications in the plants. The first implementation took 20 months from start to finish and followed a traditional phase gate or waterfall system of development in which each phase had to be completed before the next could start.

In the initial 20-month SAP implementation, the team spent nearly 3 months gathering requirements prior to starting the development and customization of the system. This meant that no custom code linking the SAP system to our other business systems was written until the requirements phase was completed. Furthermore, when the system was unveiled after months of development, the users in the plant immediately pointed out that it did not work the way they thought it would and did not meet their business needs. IT, for their part, insisted they had built the system exactly as the users told them it should work at the requirements-gathering stage.

What happened? At every step of the process the need and allowance for discovery and learning was omitted. The team finally completed the implementation but met their 20-month deliverables only through individual heroics and by reworking the system to meet the true needs of the users in manufacturing.

Later, when the team looked back on the process and analyzed its approach (using value stream mapping techniques), they found that their efforts contained as much as 80% rework because, although the initial requirements were very thorough, they had not anticipated all of the discoveries that were made later in the process.

When it came time to start on the next plant, management was looking for a better way, one that would shave considerable time off the development cycle. They turned to the same lean principles used to achieve dramatic improvements in manufacturing to help streamline development. With the help of external consultant Jim Luckman, the teams started to think about how to apply the concepts of lean to development in IT. From this initial effort the idea of fast learning cycles was born. The team's challenge was to implement SAP in the next manufacturing plant in half the time. By using the fast learning cycle approach, they not only met their goal, they beat it.

Not every developer or innovator can go to the gemba, or visit places where the principles have been put into practice, so think of this book as an expanded gemba walk through the principles of innovative lean development, showing what we believe are the best-practice behaviors currently used by professionals attempting to implement innovative lean development.

Chapter 1

The Six Principles of Innovative Lean Development

"A principle is a marvelous thing. It never changes."

Frank Lloyd Wright

As we look into examples of great development, we find that behind all examples of excellent designs there are excellent principles at work. Principles provide a framework, or a way of thinking about efficiency and completeness in design. Lean development embraces the principles of flow, pace, pitch, and the elimination of waste, all of which originate in the foundations of lean manufacturing systems. Structured innovation embraces the principle of creating innovative solutions using a standard, repeatable method.

An innovative solution is one that best meets the visible (known) and the hidden (unknown) wants of the user. It is also the simplest and most cost-effective approach, which means it reduces waste in the design from the start of the process. Innovation requires the gathering and sorting of myriad ideas in order to come up with the optimum and freshest idea in the marketplace. Any search for a new solution has an optimum answer that both maximizes the value to the user and minimizes the waste (or detractors) that the user would experience.

The Journey to Innovative Lean Development

Six principles make development both innovative and lean:

1. Identify and fill user gaps
2. Use multiple learning cycles
3. Stabilize the development process
4. Capture knowledge
5. Use rapid prototyping
6. Apply lean management principles, including learning cycles and visual boards

Identify and Fill User Gaps

The primary idea behind innovative lean development is that the final product, process, or service is an innovative solution, one that stands significantly above the other solutions in its class.

An innovative solution must meet the unspoken wants (or values) of the people who will ultimately benefit from it, that is, what is important to the customer or user. To determine what these wants are requires intensive research. The goal is to express them accurately and in a form that the design team can understand and directly apply to the project. This requires a method that allows the team to use the same vocabulary as the users when expressing the values that the solution must apply. The method must also expose the gaps between the problems and the potential solutions.

The process of fast learning cycles is designed to regularly and repeatedly bring gaps out in the open. During each learning cycle, the team discovers solutions to close the gaps, and learning cycles are repeated until the optimum solutions are found.

Use Multiple Learning Cycles

Multiple learning cycles provide a cadence, including pace and pitch, to discovery throughout the development process. Since all development is a process of discovery, development becomes a heuristic process, which means that between the initial concepts and the ultimate solution, discoveries result through a process of questioning, experimentation, and evaluation of possible answers.

The use of deliberate, repeated learning cycles allows the development team to maintain a pace while simultaneously narrowing the number of solution sets at each stage until the team arrives at the optimum answer. Thus, the learning cycles incorporate the key lean principles of pace and pitch into the development process. Breaking the discoveries into learning cycles and systematically moving through each one dramatically reduces the overall project time and improves the result.

Stabilize the Development Process

Going faster by using learning cycles and applying knowledge from previous projects will help the team, but if supporting processes slow it down, the whole development system will limp along. Therefore, a key principle of innovative lean development is to support the process of development by stabilizing and streamlining the entire development process. The main goal of development is to design a solution as quickly and efficiently as possible, which means minimizing the wastes that stand in the way of a smooth process.

Capture Knowledge

As the development team discovers solutions to the problems it is attempting to solve, the team will generate new knowledge, which should be captured and shared. Knowledge held individually does not benefit the organization. Capturing and sharing knowledge helps the organization learn from past attempts to solve problems and allows teams to accelerate discovery in the future.

Use Rapid Prototyping

All development has inherent risks. Innovative lean development reduces risk and accelerates learning by building prototypes, that is, by constructing experiments that reflect the ultimate solution and learning from them.

Apply Lean Management Principles

Finally, applying lean management principles helps to drive change through the organization. Lean management gives the organization a set of goals

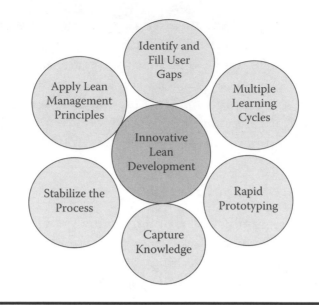

Figure 1.1   The six principles of innovative lean development.

and a purpose, which leaders can use as they strive for excellence in the development process and communicate these expectations to the rest of the organization. Applying lean management standards changes the behaviors, practices, and habits of teams. This is the only way to change the culture of a development organization. For this reason, lean must be implemented beyond the team level to all areas of leadership.

Using these principles, design teams achieve innovative outcomes because the method ensures an optimal solution to key design problems. In the process, the design team will have designed out the wastes that are universal to all designs and, by applying the key lean principles of flow and pace to the process, will have found the solution faster than using phase-gate-style development. (Chapter 3 explores the topic of learning cycles as a way to create pace and pitch in the processes of development and innovation.)

We work with teams that are on the journey to incorporate all six principles into their development process. Often one team will demonstrate a best-practice behavior, which is shared with other teams. The process of showing one team another team's progress (or benchmarking one company against one's own company) is called a gemba walk. In Japanese, gemba means "the real place." A gemba walk entails going to the actual place, seeing the actual process, and talking to the people doing the actual work. Often this is referred to as the *three actual* or the *three Ps* for place, process, and people. On a gemba walk, the students go to see the place, view the best-practice process, and talk to the real people involved in the process. Over time, the process changes are shared and disseminated throughout the entire organization. This allows the lean culture to spread.

Create a Culture of Innovative Lean Development

These six principles define a road map that all companies can apply to create a lean development culture. This change is a journey. It will not happen overnight in any organization. However, with attention to the details and by following these principles, change can be achieved. Cultural change is a difficult thing to drive. On a family trip, if the parents suddenly say to their children, "We will have a new culture of harmony in this family," in all probability nothing will change. For the children and parents to move into a new culture, the underlying behaviors must change. The children must learn to get along. The parents need to create an environment of harmony and model appropriate behavior.

So it is with any cultural shift. To change the culture in the organization, the principles for an innovative and lean culture must be nurtured and grown. The leaders need to model it, and the employees need to practice it. Over time, if the principles are followed and practiced on a regular basis, the culture will change.

Your journey can begin by learning and applying these principles within your company. To help you visualize what the future might bring, here is our vision:

- By applying the principles of innovation, expect the solutions to be unique in the marketplace.
- By implementing fast learning cycles, the solutions will be developed with less rework.
- Customers will be more satisfied because the team will have iterated more solutions and optimized multiple ideas into a solution that meets the visible and the hidden wants and needs of the customer.

Teams practicing lean development do not stop at examining only one or two ideas, but instead simultaneously explore a dozen or more ideas, which are examined in detail and documented. Of course, some concepts will quickly be deemed no-win solutions for your organization and the customer, and will be killed rapidly. However, all ideas will be visible to the entire team, and the process of learning what works and what does not will be documented as the team works through the learning cycles and regularly shares results with management.

By applying lean methods to broken process steps, the whole process becomes more efficient and effective; therefore, the speed of developing and innovating increases. One leader described his experience of moving through the early conceptual and feasibility phases of a project as "moving at lightning speed." Another business area improved its cycle time of development by over 50%, from 24 or more months to just 6 to 18 months; and the information technology teams routinely complete projects in half the time it previously took.

With the principle of knowledge capture, team members will document and share their knowledge within the team and with the broader organization; therefore, the organizational knowledge bank will increase. Teams will be able to easily go back and retrieve both ideas generated and the details on the refined solutions. It also helps to expect teams to document their solutions as part of the process, instead of at the end of the project. In this way, knowledge is captured continually as the team moves through learning cycles, and time is not wasted recreating and rediscovering what has already been learned. This boosts the productivity of the team and the organization as a whole. Management knows the progress made and will know where to go to see the results of the process.

Using the principle of rapid prototyping, learning will accelerate dramatically. Expect to work through some prototypes in a matter of days, instead of months. Also, expect to explore prototypes for many solutions, not just the favorites. Teams will reach feasible solutions much more quickly because the prototypes will be tested by the developers and validated by their ultimate users. The risks of placing untried and nonvalidated solutions in the hands of customers or users are dramatically reduced.

Finally, as leaders apply the lean management principles they will be able to monitor and assess the dimensions of innovation, learning cycles, visual controls, and knowledge capture practiced by their teams. Since what gets measured gets done, having a way to measure teams allows the leader to track the progress of projects, as well as to assess how effectively the teams have used the principles of innovation and lean development. The leader will be able to describe to the team (and with the team) areas that are doing well and areas that still need improvement. Knowing how the team rates on innovation and lean development also allows the leader to initiate process improvement activities.

Implementing major changes toward a new vision within an organization takes time and effort. The principles described in the following chapters will give your organization a head start on using a lean process to create new innovative solutions. Each step you take on the journey toward this vision will improve the effectiveness of your organization. The principles are integrated yet independent in that each has its own focus and goals. For instance, visual controls can be implemented to achieve the benefits of team accountability and increased project speed without necessarily affecting other functions.

Of course, the power of innovative lean development is realized when all of the principles are attended to and moved forward together. Although each principle is dealt with separately in these pages, when all are integrated the organization will enjoy the speed, quality, and improved cost that can be achieved by implementing innovative lean development.

Chapter 2

Facilitate Innovation with Fast Learning Cycles

"While there are many theories, techniques and tools for achieving elements of this quest, it is a journey to make innovation a systematic offering as well as 'lean from day one.'"

Bart Huthwaite, author and innovator

Innovation is the holy grail of development because innovation is what sets your product, process, or service apart. Typical development looks to satisfy expressed customer wants (or values); the goal of innovative development is to also satisfy unexpressed customer desires. By anticipating customer needs, the innovative product, process, or service adds significant value by solving a problem in a new or unique way.

How to Develop a Culture of Problem Solving

At the heart of innovative lean development is the idea of developing a problem-solving organization. Toyota, Honda, and other companies recognized as leaders in lean have problem-solving cultures. In their cultures, problems are sought out.

> *Rule of the Golden Nugget: problems are not garbage
> to be buried; they are nuggets to be mined.*

When problems are embraced and the team searches for ways to elevate and expose them, new solutions will be created. However, the golden nuggets must be sifted out of the dirt and gravel.

The Rule of the Golden Nugget applies equally well to lean cultures in both manufacturing and development. In lean manufacturing, teams are looking for the nuggets of process exceptions, because the exceptions tell us that the process is not working as expected. Something is out of its normal operating window.

In much the same way in development, the discoveries that need to be made to bring an innovative new product or service to market are simply problems that need to be solved. In the innovative lean development culture, teams are encouraged to create a clearly defined set of problem statements at the start of each discovery phase.

> *Rule of the Manageable Nugget: don't attempt
> to mine the giant nuggets first; instead mine
> the smaller, more manageable nuggets.*

The Rule of the Manageable Nugget, a corollary to the golden nugget rule, tells us to break problems down into smaller, more achievable objectives inside of a learning cycle.

In a lean manufacturing plant, everyone involved in the process is encouraged to develop "eyes for waste, and eyes for flow." This is a shorthand way to remind people to look for wastes, such as inventory, motion, rework, poor quality, and so on, and then to look for ways to make the work flow to reduce overall cycle time and to process the work in the most efficient method possible.

In lean development, teams need to develop eyes for innovation. "Seeing and hearing things with your own eyes and ears is a critical first step in improving or creating breakthrough products," according to Tom Kelley of the IDEO corporation, one of the most innovative design firms in the world.* A key step in identifying potential breakthroughs is to notice all the little things that detract from the solution.

---

* Tom Kelley. *The Art of Innovation: Lessons in Creativity from IDEO, America's Leading Design Firm*, p. 28.

Problem solving is not an event but a process; therefore the innovative organization focuses on the approach, which must be:

- Structured
- Repeatable
- Able to capture all the ideas generated throughout the process

Just as a librarian uses book call numbers to catalog all of the books, magazines, audio and visual material contained in a library, a person or a team attempting to solve a problem will generate, and need to catalog, many ideas while trying to find the ultimate solution. Each idea along the way sparks other ideas and is a building block toward the optimal solution. When a team works on a problem, and can see all of the ideas that have been posted, and members can share their ideas, the synergy leads to better ideas, and therefore the team will have a greater chance of achieving success and in a shorter amount of time.

> *The structured innovation approach brings order to idea generation and capture.*

The Role of Learning Cycles in Innovation

Innovation and lean development are closely linked through a process of discovering answers. To maximize effectiveness and ensure repeatability, innovative lean development needs a structure to help guide this discovery. In structured discovery, the smaller, manageable chunks of development are called *learning cycles*. A learning cycle is a short burst of learning in which specified problems are solved. Learning cycles must be planned and structured. To do this, start by identifying what must be learned in that short period of time. This means:

- Define the problems
- Work only on those problems
- Learn from the work that is completed
- Iterate (do it again)

When this is done rapidly, learning accelerates.

Development often is called the messy part of an organization for good reason: the task is to solve problems for which at that moment there are no answers. To do this strategically, break the problems down into smaller, manageable chunks and attack them systematically.

Fast learning cycles are 2- to 4-week development bursts that focus on specific objectives. These objectives—things the team must still discover, known as *knowledge gaps*—should be stated as problems. In innovative lean development, the goal is to apply lean principles and regularly communicate to management to keep the project moving forward.

All learning cycle thinking and communication require answers to the following questions:

- Where are we?
- Are we there yet?
- How do we get there?

These questions keep the stakeholders engaged in the project, giving real-time feedback. The answers keep the project connected to the overarching value of the project, which is, after all, the reason for putting the framework in place. If the team is not yet there, that is, if the problems have not yet been solved, the third question keeps the team thinking about how to get there. This is called *identifying the gaps*. The gaps need to be filled to maintain learning and encourage innovation.

Learning cycles lead to optimized solutions. As short development bursts, fast learning cycles lead to rapid development. Lean learning cycles add rapid iteration and a visual, structured, repeatable process to achieve results.

How to Choose the Right Problems

One reason problem statements are critical to development is that they direct the team to search for knowledge that is not currently known to the developer or to the organization.

Work on the problems that have the most impact. Set priorities in line with corporate strategy, keeping in mind various constraints. A resource constraint might be money to invest, key performance parameters, a government code or regulation, and so on. These criteria are important, and they should be clearly stated and brought to the forefront. They help to frame a problem. Without clearly stating all of the constraints of a problem, the solution is likely to be incomplete.

A typical constraint to innovation at many companies is keeping a new system compatible with the old one. One might say that a new solution must be backwards compatible. For example, if in developing a new bookshelf that connects to a panel system, several panel systems were introduced over the course of the product's development history, the shelf must interface with each of them. A key problem constraint in this situation includes:

- Which panels must the new bookshelf connect to?
- How will the connection be made?
- Can the connection be universal, or will there need to be several different connection points?

This is an example of one constraint. There will be several constraints for each problem to be solved.

This illustrates an important point: once the need is established, take the time to define the constraints of the problem. The constraints help define the gap between the problem and the solution, and filling the gaps is where innovation is needed.

Progressive development organizations add business requirements for a clearer picture of the right direction. Determining what the customer values is a crucial part of framing the problem. If a customer values low price over everything else, the team has a better picture of what is needed. If it is not price, it might be durability; if not durability, it could be maintainability. As customer values are more clearly defined, the team has much needed information on what the team hopes to develop. Huthwaite calls these the customer values, and defines them with eight categories for "problem restructuring."* Restructuring a problem involves breaking the problem down into the elements that a customer will value. As innovative development takes hold, the focus changes to one that strives to maximize all the customer values.

---

* Bart Huthwaite. *The Rules of Innovation*, p. 57.

Innovate to Fill the Gap

To be certain the right problems are worked on, the innovator should keep the goal of the customer in mind by carefully defining the customer values at the outset and should continually revisit those value statements through-out the design process. These value statements should then be turned into learning objectives for the learning cycles. Typical learning objectives for building a shelf might read like this:

- The shelf must hold 100 pounds of books and papers.
- The shelf must have a reusable label.
- The surface should be cleanable and must meet the standards of labs and hospitals.
- The materials should be "green" (environmentally friendly).
- The shelf must be knocked down (flat in a box) and ship complete.
- Assembly time should be less than 1 minute.

This end-in-view approach sets the team down the road toward satisfying the customer first. The endpoint described by the learning objectives is clear, but the path to reach it is still unclear. This gap between what is known and what is needed to solve the problem sets up the innovation process.

Spanning the gap between the goal and a set of unknown objectives requires innovation.

For example, to meet the value statements for the shelf, a whole series of unknowns requires answers:

- What materials and construction methods will support 100 pounds of books?
- What type of labeling is the customer looking for?
- What type of cleaning materials will be used?
- Will the clean environment of hospitals and labs be met?
- What materials can't be used because they are not green or environ-mentally friendly?
- How will the shelf ship? Can it ship without much packaging material to meet the green requirement?
- Who will assemble the shelf, and what tools will be available to them?

If the end is known, how is the gap spanned? What is the process used to travel across the abyss to close the gap?

Here is where the innovator steps away from attempting to get to the next level of development by building on what is already used and what is already known about how to accomplish the goal. This traditional, small-steps-forward implementation approach is common, but the solutions are generally enhancements or improvements rather than innovations. This level of activity does not drive innovation. As a result, the customer is left wanting a more complete solution, such as a jump in usability or the excitement generated by a new application or approach. Customers want innovation.

To bridge this gap and move into a space that is really innovative, development cannot take small steps forward; it must look backward from that large leap ahead. Most organizations employ only deductive thinking, or moving linearly from the present state to the future state. This results in incomplete solutions. They should also use inductive thinking, which starts with the desired future state and asks, "How can the team get there from here?"

Have you ever used the answer in the back of a math textbook to see how to solve a problem? That is inductive reasoning. It can help solve the math problem, but more important, when applied to a defined development problem, it can help solve the customer's needs and unspoken wants.

Inductive thinking allows teams to innovate
and solve business problems.

The First Critical Step: Framing the Problem

During the initial learning cycle, the development team frames the problem in a way that ensures that the gap is defined and that the right objectives are outlined. Key customer values are labeled and defined.

A strategic start takes the customer values and validates them against the customer's wishes. Equally important, existing solutions should be mapped against these values to provide early feedback on how well the team is meeting the value statements. The competition's solutions should also be measured against these values. These predictive measures of existing and competitive solutions can be further enhanced by measuring them against the potential lean wastes, including rework, waiting, and overproduction—the typical enemies of a development cycle. The challenge is to achieve the desired solution on time, with high quality, and within budget.

An important first step in the innovation process is to create a team baseline against which the values and wastes of the current product or solution is measured. From this, a clear image unfolds of how the company's existing solutions and the competitors' solutions fulfill the customer's wants and needs. The image also helps the team recognize how different solutions have been compromised or suboptimized to meet only some of the customer's needs and wants.

How To Frame the First Learning Cycle for Innovation

1. Define the problem and objectives. These learning objectives define the gap between what you want but don't have. Innovation will be used to fill the gap.

2. Label and define the key customer values. If the values are not completely known, do additional research with the user of the proposed innovation whether it is a product, process, or service.

3. Further define the gap between the customer needs and current solutions.

4. Validate your ideas for filling the gap with a customer group or with trusted representatives of the customer group.

5. Create a baseline for the existing solutions, yours and your competitors, that attempt to fill that gap currently.

6. Generate as many ideas as possible for filling the gap.

Customers live in the present, so their stated wants speak to their present problems. Encourage the team to consider the customer's future wants. What will the customer want in 2 years? In 5 years? These are the unspoken wants, and they are crucial to defining the place where the customer wants the next product to jump. This is defining the gap, where innovation lives.

Asking the customer is an excellent way to define wants, but there are other methods as well that allow the team to see the future wants of the customer. IDEO, which is known for meeting customer needs, both spoken and unspoken, utilizes user observation and behavioral research to create gap lists for innovation. Other approaches include user-centered research, utilizing marketing as the voice of the customer and the sales organization as the voice of the company. Careful listening and accurate information gathering helps the team formulate the correct target for innovation. Together, these are the start of a more unified theory of innovation.

In the next step, customer values are refined and become the target for the team. By restructuring the project in this way, the team starts with the end clearly in view. Knowing the endpoint allows the team to focus on how to get there from where it began. A review of the existing and proposed ideas generated by the team in the first learning cycle provides further definition of the gap between what the customer wants and what is currently available. Using inductive thinking, the team can work backwards and then leap forward to fill the gap. Making this leap is innovation.

The Components of Innovation

It is common to recognize the need for innovative solutions. However, what it means to innovate and what traits are common to innovators are not so clear.

A unified theory of innovation seeks to teach the methods of innovation by providing a mental framework for assembling techniques and tools in a process that enables a person to innovate. Several elements are required for successful innovation, including:

■ A method to describe the needs and features that the customer will value. This includes a method to observe user behavior to capture the unspoken wants of the audience for whom the solution will be devised. This user-centered approach is a key to defining the most innovative solutions.

■ A method for categorizing, generating, and capturing new ideas. Cataloging ideas is a crucial activity throughout the learning process. Capturing ideas provides knowledge that will be used by the innovator and the organization. In addition, a list of previously proposed ideas to solve the problem is a powerful guide for sparking other new ideas.

■ A process for measuring ideas and solutions set against the values that the customer will use when judging the solution.

■ A technique for bringing in outside perspectives and thinking. This is most important of all.

When these four elements come together, the innovator will be able to close the gap in the innovation space. The gap is closed when user needs are correctly described and carefully generated, and cataloged sets of ideas are proposed to meet those needs. Those ideas should have included outside

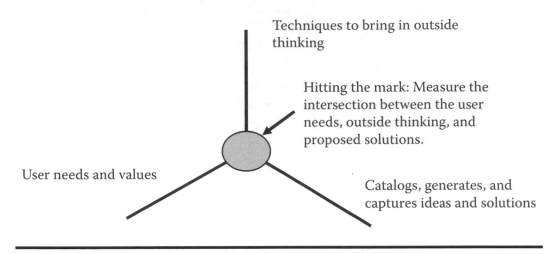

Figure 2.1   Model of a unified theory of innovation.

thinking about concepts and processes that your organization has not yet tried.

Measuring how well these come together provides an indicator of how close the innovation has come to hitting the sweet spot, or what Huthwaite calls the intersection of "three paths of knowledge."* The three arms of innovation seem to be universal, as different organizations and people have demonstrated. The first arm describes the user's wants and needs; the second branch involves idea generation and capture; and the third brings in an outside perspective.

Organizations that are highly successful innovators use the three-armed innovation process intuitively. IDEO brings in user observations to describe what the user truly needs, and relies on its diverse staff to bring in outside thinking. Prodigious brainstormers, they generate large quantities of ideas, which they number and catalog as they go. IDEO hits the sweet spot of innovation when they bring together the three arms of innovation, namely user observation, idea generation, and outside thinking, to create an award-winning solution.

Figure 2.1 describes structured innovation. Most people use an unstructured approach to innovation, which is not nearly as effective because it relies on chance, and, of course, it is extremely inefficient to leave innovation to mere chance. An approach that uses chance will omit one or more of the dimensions (or axes) of the innovation equation. By contrast, when all

---

* Bart Huthwaite. *Lean Design Solution*, p. 219.

three dimensions, or principles, are used together in a structured, collected, and unified way, they produce results.

The Rule of Backward Thinking

Structured innovation is a counterintuitive process; therefore, some may find it uncomfortable because it requires a new way of thinking. Structured innovation does not flow from a deductive or linear approach. Instead, the innovative thinker who applies the principles of the unified theory of innovation uses an inductive thinking approach to generate creative ideas and solutions. This makes the method a little more difficult to master because our logical nature does not gravitate to inductive methods.

Inventors who use the inductive and systematic innovation process create a condition in their minds that sets up the need for a solution. Moshe Rubinstein and Iris Firstenberg describe the technique this way, "Rational thinking seeks to conform; creative thinking seeks to invent."* This requires backward thinking. The innovator begins with a statement of what is wanted but does not currently exist and then seeks to work backwards systematically to the solutions that will fulfill the stated need and want.

*The innovator seeks to close the gap created in the
mind with a set of creative ideas and solutions.*

The main idea is to be explicit about the gap between the outcome and the ultimate solution, from the place where the solution is today to the place where the customer wants to be in the future. In other words, the gap must be documented and clearly stated as a problem to be solved or a potential trade-off between two key factors.

If the gap is defined and stated as learning objectives inside a learning cycle, then the mind of an inventive person will attempt to close it. Rubenstein and Firstenberg believe inventors must "hold opposites in the same space or frame long enough to permit the possible emergence of new frames, new ideas, or new creative sparks."† When the gap exists inside the learning cycle, the team will have a structured method for keeping the gap open as long as possible to find these ideas and creative sparks.

---

* Moshe Rubinstein and Iris Firstenberg. *The Minding Organization*, p. 22.
† Moshe Rubinstein and Iris Firstenberg. *The Minding Organization*, p. 25.

A lean culture contains a group of people who seek out problems while attempting to continuously improve the environment in which they work. Similarly, the innovative culture will have many individuals who continually attempt to find ways to close the gaps between the problems with innovative solutions.

Of course, remaining in a comfortable position and not stretching to innovate can easily be achieved simply by never exposing the gaps, but the innovator never rests until the gaps are exposed and finally filled. Exposing the gaps requires us to move to a new level of innovation and requires new thinking and research into areas that are not currently within our reach. It causes us to look outside of ourselves for solutions in other areas.

> *A person, a workgroup, or a company is innovative when it exposes the gaps of opportunity between customer needs and current solutions and then finds solutions to close them.*

By changing organizational behavior and practice to allow new ways of thinking about exposing and embracing the gaps, innovating teams will move away from the past culture in which exposing and leaving gaps open is viewed as failure and will move to an innovative culture that seeks out and exposes gaps in order to apply innovative thinking to close them. True innovation will occur when the creative culture is nurtured and innovative solutions are developed at every point where the organization's process touches the client.

The Role of Outside Thinking

If innovation is filling the gap between anticipated customer wants and what is available today, then the innovator is the person searching to understand what the customers want but don't have. In so doing, the innovator is setting up a leap to a future state solution and then works backwards from the stated gap.

Because innovation means working outside the normal arena of current thinking, all innovations require out-of-the-box thinking, such as looking to other industries, other products, or nature itself. The great American

---

Examples of Improbable Gaps

A CEO tells the company to make the whole showroom environmentally friendly and cradle-to-cradle certified in 6 months. *Cradle to cradle* is a term used to indicate that the materials in the product are sustainable from the birth of the product, throughout its life, to its death when it can be recycled and reused in the birth of the next product.*

An automotive executive sets the new jump in technology by giving the design team a goal of driving cross-country on one tank of fuel.†

The Progressive $10 million X-Prize is offered to the first company to reach 100 mpg to inspire a new generation of viable, super-efficient vehicles that help break our addiction to oil and stem the effects of climate change at a time when our current fleet of vehicles has an average fuel economy 21 mpg, or 4 mpg less than the Ford Model T.‡

A builder accepts a challenge to build a home that is completely off the power grid, that is self-sufficient from an energy consumption standpoint.

An office furniture company is challenged to create an office system that lays out like a cubicle, but doesn't feel like a cube, that is easy to install, able to be configured by the user, and incorporates the latest technology.

In each case, the goal initially seems impossible. That is, however, the intent of defining and stating the gap. The individuals on the team will find a way to create an innovative solution when they believe it is even remotely possible.

---

* "Steelcase Delivers Sustainable Solutions at NeoCon 2008," http://www.reuters.com/article/pressRelease/idUS138349.

† "Toyota Chief Envisions Cross-Country Trip on Single Tank of Gas," http://www.edmunds.com/insideline/do/News/articleId=106232.

‡ http://www.progressiveautoxprize.org/prize-details.

---

architect Frank Lloyd Wright used this technique with students at his Taliesin School of Architecture: every 6 months he asked them to present a "box" project, meaning to create buildings that broke through the conventional post and beam construction. For Wright, the innovative structure stretched the materials to create buildings that are open and connect the interior of the building to the outside, with nature itself.

Innovative solutions are a recombination of things in a new or unique way; by looking elsewhere, new concepts are imported into the current solution. There is nothing new under the sun, just new ways of putting them together.

Case Study: Innovation—A New Way to Put Existing Things Together

The Walkstation™ is a combination of two familiar products: a height-adjustable table that had been previously offered and a specially designed treadmill that operates only at walking speeds.* The outside thinking that brought the two together came from Dr. James A. Levine, a Mayo Clinic doctor concerned with office workers' health and fitness, who had a vision of providing them with a low-impact, low-stress way of improving their lives. Dr. Levine had done some of the prototyping using a low-speed treadmill in his office.†

The gap had been identified, setting up the potential innovative product. Working backwards, Dr. Levine needed a way to combine office furniture with sporting goods. He found an office furniture company that agreed to combine two basic products and helped turn his idea into a new marketable innovation. Dr. Levine found an idea in one setting and used it in another. That is outsight—looking outside the current industry into other industries or to nature itself.

The Role of Outsight

Innovation cannot be confined to a meeting or a time of day. Innovation is not an event. It is an ongoing systematic application of experience, envisioning the new and borrowing from the past. Huthwaite calls these foresight and hindsight. The third sight is outsight. Combined, these three sights create insight, a new way of looking at something. Albert Einstein knew the importance of using all of these sights to create out-of-the-box thinking. Einstein said, "The problems we face today cannot be solved on the same level of thinking we were at when we created them."

Typically, outsight is the least practiced of these three sights. Innovators should continually be looking to combine existing solutions in a new way, so why not use all the ideas available? Think of places Dr. Levine might have looked for his outsight. He knew treadmills had evolved from simple moving belts to machines with programmable electronic displays that even

---

* http://www.steelcase.com/na/files/c69ebbea0d2240ceb1e5fa268780b0c5/WalkstationBrochure.pdf.
† James A. Levine, MD, PhD, Professor of Medicine, Physiology and Bioengineering, and Richard Emslander, Chair of Nutrition and Metabolism, Mayo Clinic, Rochester, Minnesota.

include cup holders. What were the gaps? What about accommodating workers of different heights? What about combining other exercise equipment with a table? Dr. Levine extracted the ideas from other markets to apply to his new solution. Where would he look for office solutions?

You can see how this could snowball in a very positive way. If the inventor is concerned about height adjustability, the innovator might find possible solutions in many places. For example, the height of the cut adjustment on her push lawnmower uses a single lever; she adjusts the height of her bicycle seat with a cam-over mechanism similar to a bicycle wheel quick-release. Might either of these ideas be used to adjust the height of a table? She starts seeing ideas that she might borrow in many places. On her drive to work, while walking the dog, at the deli counter, and so on. To be useful to her and her organization later, these ideas must be cataloged, stored, and retrievable.

Systematic, structured methodology practiced by innovators is a critical part of embedding innovation into development. Experience and vision help frame a solution, but it is extracting ideas from other areas that can really accelerate the generation of innovative solutions. Outsight is seeing what is already there (but in other unrelated areas) and wondering if that might be the solution to a problem in a different setting. Initially, outsight does not seem intuitive; however, it is a basic part of innovation, and it can be developed through practice.

Focus on User Needs to Uncover Opportunities

Thinking with the end in mind is another key technique used to identify the problem and to establish the gap that exists between what the customer needs and the state of current technology in order to find a solution to the problem. As noted, a well-crafted statement of the opportunity (or problem) is required to properly set up the innovation method. However, the opportunity needs to be defined in more detail. The process of refining or further describing the learning objectives for innovation brings laser focus to the effort of generating innovative ideas.

To see the true needs of the customer or user, focus the spotlight on the customer's needs. Focusing on the needs requires some additional tools. Innovative companies and individuals utilize multiple methods to define the needs and wants of their customers.

What follows are two methods: one for IT and one for product development. Each method is an important technique in itself, but the method selected must fit the situation.

- Information technology developers need to perfect their collection of user requirements. Value stream mapping, or showing how a process flows (see Chapter 5), allows them to see the process and gather requirements.
- Designers of new products need to find the unspoken wants in a solution and in direct user behavior. Observation is a tool that allows them to uncover those desires.

These are not the only methods used to collect user needs. However, these two methods have produced repeatable results to get at the true needs.

Incorporate User Needs and Values in New Product Design

When designers approach a major new product development project, they might utilize a method developed by IDEO: in their attempt to close the gaps, ideas generated throughout a brainstorming session are cataloged and captured on sticky notes.

What is also interesting about the IDEO design process is their practice of researching user behavior through direct observation. IDEO demonstrated this technique in an hour-long spot on the television news show *Nightline*. They had been given the task of improving the everyday shopping cart. The challenge was to complete the design in under a week. IDEO observed that supermarket customers who carried a soft drink or coffee while they shopped always used one hand to hold the cup, and, when necessary, they would set the cup down on a display so they could use both hands. From this observation came the innovation to add a cup holder to the cart. How many years did shopping carts exist before they had cup holders? Probably, too many. However, the unspoken need was always there.

A gap list, a list of problems, deficiencies, or annoyances about a design, is also created. This list provides a method for tracking the potential opportunities that exist between what customers need and what they would like to experience. The gap list and direct observation are both ways to identify the left axis of the unified theory, describing what the customer needs and values.

Another method for understanding innovation opportunities is a technique called user-centered research, which is an alternative form of observing user behavior. For example, in a user-centered research approach, workers are observed (with their permission, of course) for extended periods using video cameras so that researchers can record how people actually use their space. It allows them to see how workers change and modify their space in creative ways. When common behaviors and practices emerge, they can point to a need for a new solution. This form of anthropological study, or the study of human behavior, is an effective way to identify the whole innovation space.

More conventional methods are also used to uncover user wants and needs. The marketing department can often identify opportunities, or gaps, in their product offering. The next generation of products is generated by filling these gaps. Watching to see what custom (or engineered-to-order) products are requested by customers also helps identify innovation opportunities. The custom product requested by, designed for, and sold to the customer can become a standard product as demand for it grows. Sometimes these designs are significantly different from the standard product. This is another way to capture the desire of the market for new solutions.

Therefore, when using the systematic innovation approach:

■ An excellent starting point is to create a general statement of the desired solution. This will help identify the gap between where the solution is now and where the customer wants it to be.
■ Next, map how well any existing solutions (your own as well as your competitors') fill the gap with key desired values.
■ If there are deficiencies in how existing solutions meet the desired values, the innovation opportunities have been discovered.
■ Apply outside thinking to the opportunities to generate ideas to find solutions to fill those gaps. Multiple ideas can be combined into new solutions.

Start with Innovation; Then Innovate Throughout

Innovation begins when the problem can be stated in a way that clearly defines what needs to be done. Clearly stated problems are at the heart of any lean system; similarly, the innovative lean development method starts with a well-thought-out problem statement describing what you want but don't have.

Perhaps too often we think of innovation in terms of physical things, such as the things that are done in product engineering. To innovate throughout is to embrace a philosophy of innovation that encompasses all areas of development: design, marketing, planning, supply chain, manufacturing, sales, distribution, installation, and customer service.

For this reason, innovation starts with stakeholders from each of these areas armed with a clear understanding of the total system design across the enterprise. In addition, because front-end focus drives back-end project success, the strategy must be clear as well as lean from the start.

In this fashion, innovation can come from all directions and continue throughout the entire development life cycle. Innovation cannot be scheduled; but you can create an environment for innovation. Innovation is a mind-set, an overall approach, a way of life.

Aim for Perfection with Specificity

Think of driving that new car home from the lot. You've dreamed about it; saved for it by putting away cash; and thought about the options and features. It is the big day; you go to pick up the car, and you get the car keys. You expect everything to be perfect. The dealer goes over all of the features, buttons, dials, and gadgets. You are certainly not expecting anything to be wrong.

Even new innovative designs like hybrid cars (which combine electric motors with small gasoline engines to boost the power and charge the batteries) are expected to work correctly from the start.

To get to that level of perfection, take the design parameters that the user values, and fully define what they mean. If a design variable is adjustability, for example, do not just tell the engineers and designers it needs to be adjustable. Tell them how far, how often, and the maximum amount of effort you expect from the adjustable feature. The thing that most often derails design teams is specifications that are too loose or inconclusive.

Things to consider from the outset include:

1. Customer needs:
   - Compatible with other products
   - Adjustable to meet a range of sizes

- Sustainable to meet green product considerations
- Offered in the multiple colors as defined by the customer

2. Organizational needs:
   - Profitable cost target
   - Speed to market
   - Cost of capitalization (the investment to bring the solution to the marketplace)

3. Physical needs:
   - Performance characteristics and limits
   - Space restrictions
   - Material limitations

The root causes of loose specification are: (1) the values do not make it into the final design specifications, something that requires upfront effort to move the team from squishy and soft words to more specific and descriptive attributes; and (2) values have to be validated with the team and ultimately with the customer.

Validating initial concepts of a design very early in the process is critical to launching a project in the right direction. Often, at this stage, physical prototypes cannot yet be validated; so validate using sketches if it is a physical product, or using screen shots and basic functionality if it is an IT solution. Even more important, validate the values or design attributes that have been defined. Very early in the process, listen to your customers by presenting the values to them, and asking them to clarify how the product must perform or how the service should operate. This is possible only when the attributes are specific and measurable. In Chapter 7, we describe how to bring the voice of the customer into each learning cycle using rapid prototyping and validation techniques.

When designing a new service, find ways to express the value that the service will bring, quantify the service, and then drive it home. If the service business fulfills a need in your community, try to quantify the values of the service in real numbers. For instance, if on-time delivery is the value, quantify what on-time delivery means. Does it mean within the day, or within the hour? If excellent quality merchandise is the goal of your service, define quality in terms of getting it right the first time.

The first learning cycle in the development process is an excellent time to accurately and completely define the attributes of the product or service. As the project moves through this first learning opportunity, measure the existing product and the competition's product against the standards. This removes the mystery and subjectivity from predictive measuring.

If the team cannot quite quantify all of the values that define the product or service, use the first learning cycle to collect this data. Let the customer help define and refine the measurement standards. Remember, what gets measured gets done.

> *Rule of Driving the Innovation Process Home: values defined using measurable attributes facilitate innovation.*

Table 2.1, which includes values defined for a product with specific measurable attributes, demonstrates how this works. The attributes are refined and defined to allow solutions to be mapped against them.

How to Design out Wastes

Teams must find and eliminate creators of waste (non-value-added activity) from the solutions from the start. When the common creators of waste are referenced and designed out of a new product portfolio, the result is a

Table 2.1   Values Defined Using Measurable Attributes

Performance characteristics	Resist racking to no more than 1.5 inches with a 150-pound load, top strength to 250 pounds.
Speed to market	Available in the supply chain by first ship of January 2010.
Sustainable for green design	Achieves corporate green metrics…MBDC "cradle to cradle" Version 2 certification, lead and PVC free. Meets indoor air quality requirements, etc.
User interface	Clean look, no exposed fasteners, opening force with no more than 8 pounds of effort.
Ease of assembly	Labor to assemble the product less than 10 minutes, assembly can be completed with one driver, one bit, etc.
Shipping and distribution	System functions with zero damage from shipping whether shipped packaged or blanket wrapped.
Manufacturing requirements	Manufactured on existing lean lines in the plant. Takt times defined by manufacturing, etc.

Table 2.2 Drivers of Waste

Waiting	Occurs when one or more interdependent people (or teams) with a multitude of hand-offs and interrupters are unable to continue because they are waiting for another or others to complete a task(s).
Excess inventory	Results from limited reuse of designs, unnecessarily creating the need for new parts to be designed.
Overproduction	The result of unused "bells and whistles" being designed into a solution.
Overprocessing	Happens when concepts are completed or taken to too great of a level of detail, only to be discarded later.
Defects	Occurs when solutions are reworked late in project (or in the field).
Excess motion	Result of ineffective communication, which causes flow interrupters and excess activity in an attempt to find the right answers.
Non-value-added processing	Occurs when knowledge is lost and ground is re-covered, although others know the answers.

product that is simpler to build, has fewer parts, is easier for sales personnel to specify, and is quickly installed at the customer's site. By considering potential wastes early in the design process, the final product is less complex and more robust.

Wastes are universal—the same wastes apply to any situation, whether it is manufacturing, product, or IT design (see Table 2.2). As any new situation is approached, the definitions can be customized to fit the specific circumstances, as well as the specific products and market. In other words, the wastes remain constant, but the definitions of the terms will change and adapt to describe the situation to which the solution applies.

It is important to define the wastes upfront along with the values the customer desires in the solution. This does not take much time, but it is essential, because the wastes need to be avoided at the same time the solution is being developed. In addition, if specific wastes are unacceptable, ideas can be sought to help minimize or even completely design the waste out of the process. Avoiding the wastes can drive even more efficiency into the solution.

Create a Foundation for Innovation: Embrace Ideas and Learning Cycles

To realize fully the benefits of conducting research, observing users, and defining customer values, new ideas must be harvested from the whole company. To do this, the first step is to create a receptive environment throughout the organization. As Robinson and Schroeder point out, "the real bottleneck to ideas is not usually front-line employees but the poor reception the ideas get from the organization."*

In order to create a receptive environment—one where ideas are welcome and commonplace—leaders must relinquish some control and allow the free flow of ideas. Ideas must be accepted and not shot down. Robinson and Schroeder also recommend that leaders avoid rewarding ideas; rather, the recognition of the ideas should be the reward. Of course, the best recognition is to use the ideas whenever possible.

Remember that innovation is not an on-demand activity. Innovative ideas can come at any moment whenever the exposed gap returns to the forefront of our thinking.

Innovative lean development uses the words *systematic*, *structured*, and *methodology* to provide a framework for thinking about innovation. The methodology, once learned, provides a mental reminder of the language and methods of innovation. This methodology of innovation, these learning cycles, is folded into the systematic approach to discovery.

---

* Alan Robinson and Dean Schroeder. *Ideas Are Free*, p. 99.

Chapter 3

How Multiple Learning Cycles Contribute to Innovation

"The most valuable thing about learning cycles is the fact that you have time to react because the cycles are kept short."

A Lean Development Project Manager

Development is a learning process. It can be messy because at its most basic level, it is problem solving, and you never know where the answers will take you. In addition, most development organizations are looking for things they want but don't have, including speed, to be going in the right direction, with continuous feedback and adjustment. Perhaps most important, they want to develop a culture of learning.

Eight Steps Every Learning Cycle Must Take

To accomplish this, the organization must implement learning cycles, which are a specific series of steps used to solve development problems.

Step 1: Develop a Solid Overall Project Schedule, or Block Plan

Deadlines are a reality of all development. Customers want a solution, and management wants a solution. The timing of projects is dictated in a way that is usually out of the development organization's hands. Given this reality, the team must determine the pace at which discovery must take place and work to accomplish this schedule. Setting a block plan is not optional.

Step 2: Create Cadence, or Pace

Crucial to lean thinking is the idea of pace, that is, the amount of time it takes to do something. It is best to keep learning cycles short, about 2 to 4 weeks in duration, because this allows time to adjust to the learning gained before the next learning cycle begins. As you find answers to the problems posed, use feedback opportunities structured into the learning cycle to help adjust your work toward fulfilling the project goals.

Step 3: Create a Framework

The short bursts of learning make up the framework for increasing speed, developing direction, giving feedback, adjusting the work being done, and creating a learning culture in your development organization.

Structure and methodology are essential to the process of iteration. To learn quickly, the framework must facilitate iteration in a structured way (see Appendix A). For this reason, every learning cycle should include the following:

- *Plan:* Define what you will work on and what resources will be employed
- *Design:* Propose solutions for the problems to be solved
- *Build:* Rapidly prototype, in whatever format necessary, to solicit feedback
- *Test:* Evaluate the built prototypes
- *Review results:* Summarize what has been learned and update stakeholders

Step 4: Create an Environment of Team Participation

The development team task is to solve the problems in front of them; however, implementing learning cycles is a new approach for many of the teams. Just as team ownership is required for development success, team participation is required for learning cycle success.

Step 5: Define Objectives with Good Problem Statements

Objectives in learning cycles are statements of the problems to be solved. As with any problem, a good problem statement goes a long way toward defining the work to be done. Time used to properly frame the things to work on is time well spent.

Step 6: Keep Options Open with Multiple Concepts

A common trait of development organizations is to lock onto a single solution and chase it as far as possible. In innovative lean development, it is important to resist the urge to focus on a single solution too early. Carry as many viable solution options forward as possible, eliminating them only when necessary. This gives the organization other options if things do not go as planned.

Step 7: Use Extensive Checklists

Most development efforts have points within the development cycle that require approval. These are great times to check your progress. In addition, checklists tied to the approval process help to ensure that development teams are working toward the correct goals. Innovative lean development encourages more and better communication between these formal approval times.

Step 8: Tie Teams Together with Integration Events

Development should not operate in a vacuum, but sometimes it feels like it does. Different parts of the team, or different teams working on separate areas of the same project, can seem disconnected. As part of innovative lean development learning cycles, use regular, scheduled connection points across the entire team—or integration events (covered in the last section of this chapter)—to get everyone on the same page.

How to Develop Solid Block Plans

Many factors affect when projects begin and end. Business conditions, competition, and industry trade shows all loom large in the development of new products or services. That deadlines create the team's target is nothing new. Their purpose is to set a pace at which discovery must occur.

As an innovative lean development organization, the goal is to accelerate the learning. Projects have deadlines, but the learning cycles into which the project is broken are more focused. Most development organizations have a tollgate or checkpoint system for checking the project's status and progress. Tooling may be approved, remaining schedules inspected and adjusted, and so forth. These existing system stops are times to engage management for project evaluation and should be embraced. Do not underestimate the power of keeping stakeholders in the loop.

Set Milestones

Project milestones are important touch points, but they are typically set too far apart. An important part of a lean strategy is frequent interaction with the project stakeholders. A great practice is to develop intermediate milestones that can help keep the project on course. Figure 3.1 illustrates a project moving through many iterations, or learning cycles, during its early phases. When learning cycles are kept short (only 3 to 4 weeks long), the team can iterate repeatedly, and the end of each learning cycle provides an intermediate milestone that the team can use to check its progress, thus helping to keep the project on course. The goal is to complete as many learning cycles as possible prior to executing the solution without rework, which is called flawless execution.

Arguably, the most important milestone is the implementation phase kick-off. Development is complete, no more design changes are allowed, and execution of the project begins. The last thing any project can afford is changes at this point. A major development waste is rework, and changes after this milestone create tremendous rework. What every organization strives for here is flawless execution. The innovative lean development structure can help deliver this.

Every project has a deadline to deliver the project. Based on that end date, the project team needs to set the pace for learning. If the team works backwards from the flawless execution milestone, it can determine the time left for discovery. Discovery, or what needs to be learned, is divided into short learning cycles, which, in turn, are focused on the milestone dates.

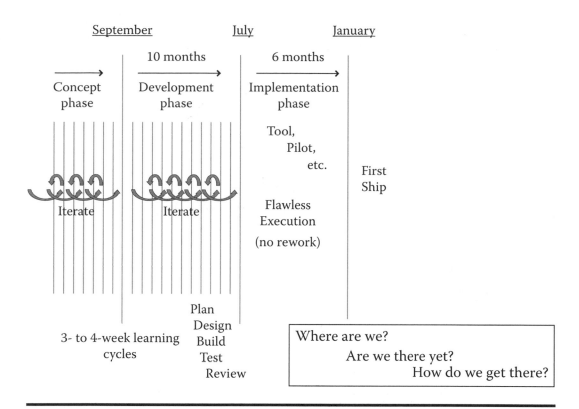

Figure 3.1 The phases and learning cycles in the development process.

Establish Objectives

As the project team develops these intermediate milestones, divide the project's goals into objectives. Objectives are the knotty parts of the project— the things to be learned in order to achieve the project's goal of meeting the customer's needs and wants.

To meet this goal, all objectives need to be solved. As a team, form questions around the unknowns that need to be answered in order to learn what is missing. The questions drive the team's individual tasks, which then drive innovation and discovery.

Any project requires block planning to deliver the project on time. This means that, given an end date:

- Set the pace at which discovery must take place.
- Work backwards from the flawless execution milestone.
- Use checklists for intermediate milestones.
- Divide objectives and questions into short learning cycles to achieve milestone dates.

When lean tools are used, the management of these steps is made visual through use of a visual board (see Figure 4.2 in Chapter 4) that can be monitored by management, project leadership, or anyone interested in the project. This closes the loop and helps deliver accelerated learning and faster organizational development.

How To Create Cadence, or Pace

Pace is a measure of getting things done based on a predefined set of ideas. For instance, when we first proposed writing this book, the publisher said that the time was ripe and that the draft should be ready by a date in the not-too-distant future. To reach that date, we needed to define a pace, which we determined was to write a section about every day.

In manufacturing, this is called the takt time. *Takt* is a German word that describes a constant beat, like the beat produced by a metronome that a musician uses when practicing difficult and rhythmic patterns. There is no natural takt time in development, so the team and its leadership have to impose the pace on the development cycle.

*Create pace at the learning cycle level to
finish the overall project on time.*

Ultimately, the principle is that tasks are measured against their due dates to see if they are completed by the predetermined project dates. For this reason, never plan to finish on time; always plan to finish ahead of time. Pace is the amount of time it takes to complete tasks, and it is more than just reaching the next milestone in a project.

The key differentiator between traditional phase gate process (the upper half of Figure 3.2), and lean development (the lower half) is that pace is applied to the learning itself. In a learning cycle, the amount of time available is purposely divided, breaking a large project into very small learning chunks, each with its own timeframe. The goal is to complete the entire

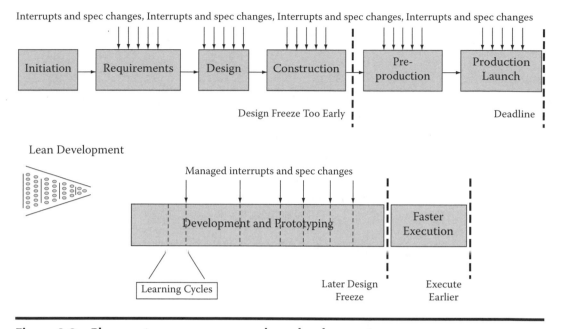

Figure 3.2 Phase gate processes versus lean development.

learning cycle including the generation of multiple innovative concepts, building prototypes, and testing them, within a preset time frame.

Each learning cycle should have well-defined objectives with questions tied to tasks. One way to do this is to ask, at the beginning of the learning cycle, such questions as what are the things that are not known, what needs to be learned about this problem, and what questions can be formulated about the problem.

Once the objectives and questions are stated, the tasks can be planned. The tasks should be assigned dates that spread out the activities to establish pace. This is the number one weakness seen in teams. It is difficult for teams to think about the subtasks that need to be accomplished. It is much easier to put down a due date. For example, to answer a learning question, some tasks should be due tomorrow, some the next day and the next, and so on. Those tasks should be completed on time to keep the learning cycle on track. The same model applies to issues. A wonderful way to maintain pace is to place tasks on an accountability board (see Chapter 8).

How do you know how long a learning cycle should take to complete? While it is difficult to determine upfront how many learning cycles will be needed or how long each one should be, the team can use the project block plan as a road map. Based on the collective experience of the team, and leaning heavily on the project manager, make the best estimate of the number and duration of learning cycles required for the current project phase.

We have talked about thinking and working backwards; the way to lay out the learning cycles is the same. The team must first understand where it needs to be for flawless execution and determine the project checkpoints between here and there. Next, based on the team's experience of what needs to be learned, split the time between checkpoints into the greatest number of learning cycles possible.

The best time to define the length and amount of time involved in each learning cycle is at the start of that learning cycle. Within each phase of the project, you should not look too far down the development path, because you will not know what additional learning is needed until the current learning is completed in the present learning cycle.

To maintain development pace, never move the end date of the learning cycle once it is set. Set the date and don't be late.

Lock your dates down, and don't let them shift. Treat them like critical events. Does the date of the Super Bowl for NFL football ever move? Do presidential election dates move? No. These dates are set a long time in advance. Similarly, each learning cycle is given an end date. Within the learning cycle, the team is asked to set up a series of learning events to answer key questions and problems and to set fixed dates in a very short time horizon for when a particular learning can be completed.

Two things happen when you lock down the learning cycle end date. First, the team is more likely to strive to complete the learning within the time allotted if there is a due date. Second, even if the team does not finish, there will still be significant learning that should be captured. This learning is what allows the team to understand the direction the next learning cycle should take. Even partial learning is better than delayed learning.

Another key reason to set the pace through learning cycles is that it gives the team a chance to hold the interrupters at bay while the team completes a development task. Interrupters come from many sources as a team navigates its way through the project. New requirements cause the team to second-guess its original assumptions and direction. Changing specifications can come to the team in many forms. Even market validation, which is very healthy (see Chapter 7), may cause the team to change direction.

The goal of learning cycles is to hold off these interrupters so that the team can complete the learning that was defined at the start of the cycle.

The project manager plays a crucial role in this process. A key activity during the learning cycle is to keep track of the interrupters so they are not lost. At the end of the cycle, all of the interrupters can be brought in and the team can deal with them at the transition from one learning cycle to the next. By doing this, the development team can learn what it needs to about the already defined problems. Distractions only cause rework, and rework costs time and money. If the team sets the learning cycle durations short enough, this approach maximizes learning and advances better solutions, no matter what the interruption may be.

Setting the pace of the project through short bursts of learning allows the organization to pull together on a short-range tangible goal, even though the overall product might be very wide in scope and stretch out over many, many months. The team's confidence in what can be learned and solved in 12 months may be fuzzy, but the team can certainly tell you if it will complete the next learning cycle in 3 weeks.

Finishing on time is usually non-negotiable, so the preliminary learning cycles schedule needs to be set at the beginning of the project. This block plan can be adjusted as the team learns more, but the end date cannot move.

As we've seen, lean thinking includes the idea of pace, the amount of time it takes to do something. The development team needs to become comfortable with the idea that timing must be checked regularly. As the team finds answers to the problems posed, feedback opportunities structured into the learning cycle help adjust the work toward fulfilling the project goals.

How to Create a Framework for Learning Cycles

Learning cycles are a fundamental principle of lean development. The way to create a learning organization and develop knowledge faster is to use the innovative lean development method to define the learning. This means that a learning cycle must be broken down into a repeatable and systematic process to ensure that all of its components—plan, design, build, test, and review the results—are present in every learning cycle. Your organization might customize the words for your process, but the intent is always the same: to move rapidly through these steps with your development team.

Although it is exciting to be part of the process of innovation in an organization, structured discovery is crucial, since organizations have little appetite for delayed product launches or budget overruns.

There are at least two possible ways to approach learning cycles. One approach is to assign each undefined problem to an individual responsible for completing the learning cycle to resolve the problem. When there are multiple problems (and of course there usually are several unsolved issues or problems), each one is given to an individual to resolve within a learning cycle. This approach might be too resource intensive; a better approach might be to include multiple learning objectives in one learning cycle and then iterate from one learning cycle to the next in rapid succession during the development phase of the project.

Map the Learning Cycle

In managing learning, the more often a project manager checks on the project's status, the better able you are to adapt plans and deliver the desired outcome. To do this, the team should develop, check, and adjust the following on a regular basis:

Plan

- Review project charter with leadership
- Define the gaps in order to close them
- Confirm commitment to the plan
- Use questions to evaluate the learning cycle based on the project's objectives
- Update the block plan
- Pull in key project activities (tollgates, etc.)

Design

- Develop a concept selection vehicle
- Define set-based concepts
- State your learning objectives
- List questions requiring answers (what, how, when, where)
- Tie questions to tasks and assign them to team members

Build

- Create prototypes
- Create an accountability board for task completion

Test

- Evaluate the prototypes
- Provide for customer validation
- Evaluate task results

Review

- Assess prototypes across the team and with management
- Evaluate concepts; narrow them, if appropriate
- Document the knowledge gained
- Identify remaining gaps to be filled; these feed the next cycle
- Manage flow interruptions and assign to appropriate person/team for resolution

This map for a single learning cycle, described in Figure 3.3, should be repeated and continued until all objectives are met and the gaps are filled. It requires discipline and structure, but the results are impressive.

Develop the Plan

Every journey starts out with a plan or a map, and a learning cycle is no different. Each learning cycle starts out with a planning phase to define what

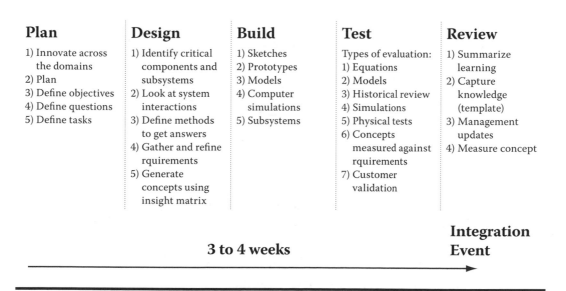

Plan	Design	Build	Test	Review
1) Innovate across the domains 2) Plan 3) Define objectives 4) Define questions 5) Define tasks	1) Identify critical components and subsystems 2) Look at system interactions 3) Define methods to get answers 4) Gather and refine rquirements 5) Generate concepts using insight matrix	1) Sketches 2) Prototypes 3) Models 4) Computer simulations 5) Subsystems	Types of evaluation: 1) Equations 2) Models 3) Historical review 4) Simulations 5) Physical tests 6) Concepts measured against rquirements 7) Customer validation	1) Summarize learning 2) Capture knowledge (template) 3) Management updates 4) Measure concept

3 to 4 weeks

Integration Event

Figure 3.3   Detail of the learning cycle process documenting each step.

the team will work on. Planning the learning objectives is a cross-functional activity, in which all disciplines are represented. The disciplines will vary depending on the type of project (for instance, IT development will have very different representation than product development projects). However, a common thread is the inclusion of the customer's voice. A customer voice on the team is critical to sorting out the true requirements, and helps when it comes time to make trade-offs.

Planning should occur in the very first day or two of the learning cycle. When planning, the team must first capture the key learning objectives. An objective is something that needs to be discovered, essentially, a problem statement. Next, for every learning objective, the team should write down all of the questions that need answering to determine what it is that the team does not know yet. The questions are all of the things that are not currently known, but need to be answered within the learning cycle. These questions will close the gap between where you are and where you wish to go.

The objectives and questions should be outlined in a 1- to 2-hour planning session at the start of each learning cycle. The members of the team should also start to think about the tasks that will need to be completed to answer the questions. These become the tasks on the accountability board for the learning cycle.

Objectives, questions, and tasks should all be linked.

Some teams use a numbering scheme; objective one will spawn several questions, and each question will spawn several tasks.

Objective 1

Question 1.1	Question 1.2	Question 1.3
Task 1.1.1	Task 1.2.1	Task 1.3.1
Task 1.1.2	Task 1.2.2	Task 1.3.2
Task 1.1.3	Task 1.2.3	Task 1.3.3
Etc.	Etc.	Etc.

This clearly demonstrates a key principle: the objectives, questions, and tasks are all interrelated; thus, there are:

- Learning objectives with specific measurable outcomes
- Questions with owners assigned (multiple questions per objective)
- Tasks with owners (multiple tasks per question)

At this point, there is an opportunity to integrate innovation into the planning. The planning meeting should include a step in which the customer values are defined in more detail. Detailed value statements help make the goals for the customer explicit. Key attributes, such as performance, affordability, and serviceability, should be stated and accurately defined for your design. This crucial step will help the team accurately compare designs against the values of the customers.

Planning and Resource Management

All development requires a wise distribution of human, financial, and other resources. However, all companies face the same challenge: to get results and finish projects with limited resources. A study by the National Center for Manufacturing Sciences found that lean automotive companies like Toyota, Honda, and their suppliers have dramatically better results utilizing their resources to hit their development targets than other companies. The study noted that*:

■ Lean companies take half the time their nonlean competitors take to reach the market with their products.
■ Toyota is nearly four times more productive than some of its competitors are. For example, Toyota assigned 150 product engineers to a car program compared to 600 for Chrysler (which took twice as long).

Clearly, additional resources alone do not ensure higher quality results, faster answers to problems, or a quicker response to market demand. However, following the principles of innovative lean development, the goal should always be to move from an environment where engineers, designers, and programmers spend only 20% of their time on value-added activity (the average for many U.S. companies) to a lean model in which up to 80% of their time is devoted to value-added activities.

A successful model for resource management includes a flexible human resource pool that can be called on for spikes in development activity. Each cycle requires actions to speed development along, but each cycle requires different and unique resources as the problems and the focus change.

---

* NCMS Study, "Product Development Process—Methodology & Performance Measures Final Report," January 31, 2000.

As the pace of discovery increases, flexibility of resources is essential. Organizations that plan for this and execute well will be ahead of the game.

> *Rule of Resource Flexibility: in order to achieve innovation and problem-solving flexibility, resources must be flexibly managed.*

The flexible resource model calls for planning for resources at the start of each learning cycle. Since the learning objectives are determined at the start of each learning cycle, the resources required become visible and can be flexed and changed. The problems that are defined will direct the team along the proper discovery paths, and planning will help the team's management identify what resources should be applied. The key is to apply resources only for as long as they are actually required.

Consider the upfront phase of a large IT project. The team identified a long list of feasibility questions relating to the various options for handling the business problems encountered in manufacturing scheduling. Using the rule of resource flexibility, the team brought in an IT consultant for just a few days to answer the questions that they had prepared at the beginning of the learning cycle. This was a huge improvement over the previous practice of hiring an IT consultant for months, during which time the team asked questions one-by-one over an extended period.

Still, there are times when a series of large and difficult problems must be solved. Although large and complex problems require a focused effort, resources can remain flexible. In such cases, the ultimate flexible model—*swarming*, in which many resources are brought in for a short period to complete all of the assignments and answer all the development questions at hand—should be applied. The idea is to bring in the right resources for the right amount of time in order to solve the problems in record time.

In the swarming phase, the resources are also pulled in to help define and refine the problem statements. Learning objectives are defined, and a list of questions is developed at the beginning of the swarming phase. These become part of the learning cycle definition, and the carefully crafted problem statements and questions bring laser focus to the problems.

> *Rule of Laser Focus: allow the team to define the problems before they attempt to solve them.*

After all, a qualified team is the best set of people to define the innovation opportunity and to solve it creatively.

Develop the Design

The time to revisit the team's assumptions and requirements is at the start of each learning cycle, and, based on the validation and research done in the previous learning cycle, ask, "What did we learn in the last learning cycle about the customer's wants (spoken and unspoken)?" The answer to that question helps refocus your direction. The team may need to adjust its definitions of the requirements. As the requirements are refined, add specificity with real numbers.

If your initial requirement was merely, "the customer wants a more efficient light source," as the learning cycles progress keep refining that requirement. What does more efficient mean? Can you express that in terms of power saved? Or the number of Kilowatt-hours saved? Or, better yet, can you express it in terms of how much money the customer will save over the life of the product? Seek to refine the requirements, even before you start.

In the experience of moving from the incandescent lightbulb to low-power fluorescent replacement bulbs, what catches our eye? It is not just the claim that it will save money per day, but the savings projections expressed per year. For example:

- ENERGY STAR–qualified bulbs use about 75% less energy than standard incandescent bulbs and last up to 10 times longer.
- Save about $30 or more in electricity costs over each bulb's lifetime.
- Produce about 75% less heat, so they're safer to operate and can cut energy costs associated with home cooling.
- Are available in different sizes and shapes to fit in almost any fixture, for indoors and outdoors.*

After the planning, the team seeks to answer the questions created at the start of the learning cycles. The key is to design more than one solution. Team members should use their innovative thinking skills to create multiple ways in their attempt to answer the questions. Designs can be simple hand sketches or a drawing of basic functional physical prototypes. Remember the goal is to create ways to test your hypothesis as quickly as possible. This is the time to break the larger solution into its smaller parts, or subsystems. For

---

* http://www.energystar.gov/index.cfm?c=about.ab_index.

example, if you are developing an IT solution, your design within a learning cycle might focus on a specific subsystem, not the whole system.

Product development and IT teams share a common need, which is to break down large projects into smaller elements. For example, if the product team is designing a new bicycle, the subelements might be grouped into three elements: (1) the frame, seat, and handlebars; (2) the wheels and brakes; and (3) the gear system. Each subelement team has specific problems to solve with respect to that element, and each element will need to connect with the others. Later, the subteams bring their subelements back to the whole system for integration.

If the IT team needs to design a new ATM machine, the team might logically organize the elements around several key subsystems: (1) the communications link, (2) the deposit and withdrawal mechanisms, (3) the display screen, and (4) the software to interact with the device.

Given all of these elements, tracking across all parts of the system is crucial. The readiness of each area to proceed is based on whether or not it is completed.

A visual control method to track the various subsystems is invaluable. The expected completion date is indicated by the number of the learning cycle in which the subsystem should be completely defined.

Element	Mechanical	Electrical	User Interface	Security	Bank Links
Process Readiness	LC1 GREEN	LC1 GREEN	LC3 GREEN	LC2 GREEN	LC3 GREEN
System Readiness	LC1 GREEN	LC1 GREEN	LC3 GREEN	LC2 RED	LC3 RED
Testing Readiness	LC2 GREEN	LC2 GREEN	LC3 RED	LC4	LC4
Training Readiness	LC3 GREEN	LC3 GREEN	LC4	LC4	LC4

Figure 3.4   Visual control method for creating an ATM; green means "ready," red "not ready." The development status of each is readily seen.

In the ATM development cycle (see Figure 3.4), the visual shows that the development cycle was progressing nicely until learning cycle 2. The cell is red, meaning "not ready," indicating problems in the security subsystem. In a case like this, the team would use the issues list for the project to capture the problem and the action items needed to correct it and get it back on track. Additionally, the visual shows the team experienced problems in learning cycle 3, where the user interface is not ready for final testing and the electronic bank link is not completed. Because the tracking method is visual, the team can see at a glance exactly where it has run into problems.

Figure 3.5 is a graphical representation of how many concepts are carried forward through each phase of development. The more concepts the team can carry forward, the more possible it is to freeze the final design as late as possible, and the more robust the solution will be.

By applying some of the techniques described earlier—insight: hindsight, foresight, and outsight (see Chapter 2)—multiple concepts can be generated quickly. The project leader should frequently remind team members to look

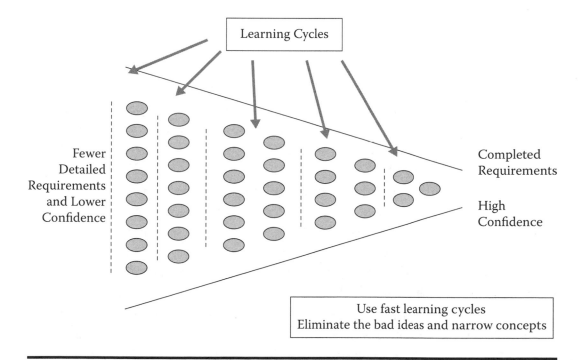

Figure 3.5   Multiple concepts narrowed through learning cycles.

outside of their own experience and knowledge base to import innovative ideas. For example:

- Suppliers can be a great source of ideas. They may already have an idea on the shelf that could be adapted to create a very innovative solution.
- Internal experts should be utilized. Keep a list of experts who can be called upon to generate innovative ideas.
- Outside services provide a rich seedbed when the team is researching into areas that are new or less familiar.
- Contract with outside service companies to generate ideas on a pay-for-service contract.

These are all great ways to round out the team's innovation idea bank; just be sure to appropriately protect the interest of all parties as the team finds and uses these rich outsights. The goal is to revisit the innovation ideas at the start of each learning cycle with as many sources of outsight as possible by focusing the ideas around the problem and questions that require answers.

Build and Prototype

Once the solutions are planned and the designs for rapid prototypes are created, it is time to test the theories with real working prototypes. The number one way to reduce the risks in development is to create prototypes that test the questions enumerated at the start of the learning cycle. (For more on prototyping, see Chapter 7.)

To be successful, the project leader should urge the design teams to prototype rapidly, in whatever format necessary, to solicit feedback on the proposed direction. Simple wood models work very well for physical product prototypes. Even mechanisms can be prototyped with simple models. Some teams have gone as far as to build an entire lean manufacturing line by laying it out in 3D with cardboard and foam pieces.

IT systems can be prototyped just as well as physical items. The team should start with prototypes based on out-of-the-box functionality. Next, the team can move to screen simulations. Later, automation can be added. It should not be added at the beginning since automating something before it is a known solution is the sort of waste lean development is trying to avoid.

Mary and Tom Poppendieck call this type of rapid prototyping agile software development.* The concept involves breaking down the larger designs into subsystems. In the learning cycle approach, cycles should be defined based on critical subsystems. My kids have tried this riddle on me: "How do you eat an elephant?" The answer: "One bite at a time." We apply similar thinking in innovative lean development. The lean development question, which is not a joke, is, "How do you conquer a large system project?" The answer: "One subsystem at a time."

Larger teams and projects should be divided into their own subteams. Each team will have its own objectives and will operate at its own pace. However, once launched on their own paths, to keep parallel teams from going off track, it is important to remember that parallel teams that have their own learning cycle cadence should be in constant communication with the other subsystem teams.

Communication is critical. When multiple teams are working in parallel, the danger is that they will be waiting for each other's outputs. Therefore, back at the planning phase, the project manager must make sure that the plans are coordinated, and that the teams are communicating back and forth, as they go through their learning cycles.

It is also essential to manage cross-team issues and flow interrupters. Since pace is a driver, the project manager should make sure that the teams are managing their time to finish on time, or better yet ahead of time. Elevate the interrupters and make sure that a governance process is in place to make decisions rapidly enough to keep the cadence. Flow interrupters that will prevent the learning cycle from completing its tasks should be delayed until the end of the learning cycle. Interrupters are managed on the team level by recording the interrupters and elevating them to the team leadership, communicating the issues and resolving them quickly.

The First Rule of Cadence: to finish ahead of time, manage the flow interrupters to fall between learning cycles.

Test the Result

Once subsystem prototypes are constructed, the next step is to test the result. Testing can take many forms. However, in this type of rapid learning

---

* Mary and Tom Poppendieck. *Lean Software Development: An Agile Toolkit.*

cycle development, the goal is to test only for the learning that is sought at the end of the particular cycle.

The method is very much like the method practiced by scientists around the world. A sound experiment starts out with a hypothesis statement (equivalent to stating the learning objective in the plan stage of the learning cycle). The next step is to design the experiment (the design phases in learning cycles). Once designed, the experiment must be carefully built so that it proves the hypothesis conclusively, by excluding external factors that might disturb the main variables being studied (equivalent to building prototypes). Then, the experiment is repeated to gather the data. This is the time in the learning cycle to carefully assess the objectives with experiments, testing, and evaluation of the prototypes.

These tests do not need to be overly complex. Often the simplest tests tell the most. The test should match the learning. If the prototype involves writing a software program, at this stage the program is tested to see if it is operating as designed. If the prototype involves a physical artifact, then the performance, either physical or visual, of the object is tested. The data collected are shared with the project team.

Testing should also involve users in order to validate the design. If software is being developed, take the time to show it to the key users to see if it will meet their needs. If it is a product solution, bring in customers and marketing to see how close the object comes to meeting expectations.

Testing is done in every learning cycle. This is a key difference between learning cycles and phase gate or waterfall development. Learning cycles require testing in every cycle, while traditional phase gate development waits until the "testing phase" to test for results. As many of us have experienced, waiting to test until this phase is far too late since there is no time to react and still stay on schedule. Testing at the learning cycle level gives the design team confidence that the new product will meet expectations.

Testing in every cycle reduces risks in your development process.

An important exercise at this point is to compare the test results against the requirements. Return to the values that were defined upfront. How well will the design meet those requirements? Also, check the design against the creators of waste. Has the design introduced any un-needed effects that should be designed out?

Review Results

Since the team has gone through the effort in the learning cycle to plan, design, build prototypes, and then test for the best fit with the customers, it is very important not to miss the opportunity to capture the results. Just as scientists publish the results of their experiments so that other scientists can validate their findings and build on them for future knowledge, learning cycle participants are encouraged to do the same. This is an easy step to omit, but don't. Be sure to capture all of the knowledge and learning.

The end of the learning cycle is an opportunity to summarize the knowledge gained, communicate with the team, and update the project stakeholders. Al Ward, of the University of Michigan, actually called lean development *knowledge-based development*. Capturing knowledge is at the heart of the Toyota development system. The Toyota know-how database is a well-documented repository for product knowledge, process knowledge, and development checklists (see Chapter 6 for more detail on capturing knowledge). The end of the learning cycle is one point (but certainly not the only time) when knowledge can be captured.

The Role of Pitch

The learning cycle objectives, questions, and tasks are the way we define the pace of the project, or how long it takes to do the work. Pitch is the measure of how often you check on the work, and it adds a necessary and distinctive technique to the development process.

For example, in lean manufacturing, if a process produces a part at a regular interval (for example, every minute), the pitch might be set at 20 minutes, or every 20 parts. Every 20 minutes, the leader of the line will check to ensure that the process is producing 20 parts every 20 minutes. If more than 20 parts were produced, the line is working too fast. However, if less than 20 parts were produced, the line has not met the pitch. Either way, adjustments are made every 20 minutes to keep the line on track to produce the correct number of parts per hour, shift, day, week, etc. Setting the right pitch gives you the ability to adjust to the conditions while avoiding major disruption to the schedule and, ultimately, your customers.

Applying a regular and repeatable pitch to development is a key concept in innovative lean development. Your organization already employs a type of pitch in its development; it is the tollgate or phase gate in your process. If we use these tollgates as the pitch, however, we have placed tremendous risk on our process. The length of the learning cycle provides a much better pitch for development. At the end of each learning cycle the team and its management checks on the progress by reviewing what was learned and what still remains to be done.

Each learning cycle may vary in length, but no learning cycle should extend beyond 30 days (except in rare, unavoidable occasions when complex tooling or outside resources might be involved). Due to prototyping variation, earlier learning cycles can be shorter, some only a day or 2, while later learning cycles stretch to 3 or 4 weeks. The team should keep pitch in mind when laying out the project block plan, and set the shortest time reasonably possible for pitch.

At its heart, monitoring pitch is an improvement technique. In all cases, the reason for measuring pitch is to understand the reasons for any misses, to help diagnose the process, and to look for ways to improve it. When the pitch is missed, it exposes an opportunity to examine what is wrong in the process. If the wait between examinations is too long, the team might be well down the wrong road, resulting in the ugly waste of rework. The right pitch is needed to adjust the direction of the team when it is much less costly to do so.

Another important way to maintain pitch and pace is by ensuring that the learning cycles regularly intersect. Each team will have learning cycles of different lengths as well as a different number of cycles over time, but at the end of the period, the project manager must make sure the teams come together. The intersection point is called the integration event (see the last section of this chapter).

How to Create an Environment of Team Participation

Most development organizations use project teams comprised of members from the stakeholder disciplines, and for good reason. The cross-functional development team is one of the most efficient means to make decisions and move forward. The act of creating a cross-disciplined team does not alone ensure that the team will create a winning product. Multidisciplined teams are formed to produce, but projects are successful only when all the disciplines are working together.

Optimizing performance in teams is some combination of both science and art. All teams must work together to be successful. This seems obvious, but efficiency and communication must go hand-in-hand. This relationship is crucial to our development success.

Team communication is elemental to the efficiency model. Remember, the goal is to increase the speed and improve the direction by using learning cycles. Therefore, the team must be in a position to accurately reflect the status of the project at any time. Communication among team members must be complete and timely. Ultimately, this communication during and between the learning cycles is the vehicle for effective project management.

One important element is regular and robust communication among team members. Another requirement is frequent communication between the team and management. Management is interested in project progress, but, all too often, the updates are too far apart. Here comes pace and pitch again. How long can management afford to wait before it has an opportunity for feedback? How far down a path can the project go before management can adjust direction?

Remember that learning cycles are modeled on a repeating pattern of plan, design, build, test, and review results. Leadership must be engaged in all aspects, but now the focus is on testing and reviewing results. Anyone who is a decision maker must be part of the testing. It is what drives the right solutions.

Frequent management review reaps multiple benefits. It builds discipline and responsiveness into the process, creates organizational clarity of direction, and, with more frequent input, gains the support of executives. To accomplish this, leaders must walk the process regularly. By scheduling weekly management working sessions at the project visual control boards, building regular, structured meetings into the project for feedback. All of these will drive improvement.

Management will set the tone for lean innovation. Ask the right questions and they will drive behavior (see Chapter 8, for the questions that a leader might ask). The principle is that leader engagement drives project success. Communication between disciplines may require a more open, perhaps a more vulnerable atmosphere. Accountability will drive better results faster, but accountability needs to be culturally acceptable. Team members will need a strong leadership component on which to model behavior. Feedback is crucial to success, so make feedback easy to give and easy to take. Driving continuous improvement requires it, and your development organization will be richer for it.

This is more than just geography and location, more than meetings and updates. This is an overarching, philosophical approach to getting teams talking, trusting, and helping each other. Successful innovation and development will not happen in a vacuum. Management, at its best, removes the obstacles for success. Embedding innovation and driving development already have many natural obstacles. Employ effective communication and management involvement to drive out the avoidable obstacles. It is a cultural thing, and management drives culture.

How to Define Objectives with Good Problem Statements

A learning cycle moves the developer from the unknown to the known, from things not understood to understanding. Development activities cannot be predicted and are difficult to map with complex, interdependent project management schedules because the process of moving from the unknown to the known involves activities that have not yet been imagined by the developer. Development is a discovery process and demands a heuristic problem-solving approach. Heuristic problem solving is experimental and makes use of "trial-and-error methods through the process of relating exploratory problem-solving techniques that utilize self-educating techniques (as the evaluation of feedback) to improve performance."* A developer might describe the heuristic process by saying, "I don't know what I don't know," which means, "I know the problems that I have to solve, but I don't know the answers to those problems yet."

This process of discovery makes product development both rewarding and stressful. The goal of the learning cycle approach is to make the discovery process systematic and less stressful. Synthesizing learning cycles down to a set of specific objectives helps to remove stress by clearly defining the problems that lay at the heart of the discovery process. Remember the Rule of the Golden Nugget: problems are not garbage to be buried; they are nuggets to be mined.

In the learning cycle, the goal is to elevate the learning objectives to ensure that learning and discovery take place. In fact, the pace of the project should not be measured by how many project tasks are completed on a project management chart; instead, it should be measured by the amount of learning that has been achieved and how completely and accurately the objectives have been answered. To do so, the objectives must be clearly stated in a way that allows comparative measurement. A comparative

---

* http://www.merriam-webster.com/dictionary/heuristic.

statement—as one option versus another—is likely to be effective. For example, if the problem involves designing a more fuel-efficient engine for an automobile, the learning cycle objectives could be stated as:

- Determine the engine power required versus the amount of fuel consumed to achieve of 40 mpg or more.
- Determine the fuel options versus regular octane fuels available to achieve 40 mpg or more.

Such objectives do not lend themselves to yes or no responses. They require that the designer do additional research, prototyping, and testing.

Objectives like these are exactly what Henry Ford used in designing the Model T automobile. The original 1908 Model T side-valve four cylinder engine produced 20 horsepower, and it had excellent fuel efficiency of 25 mpg (source: www.ford.com). In fact, it was the first flex fuel engine, running on either gasoline or ethanol. The Model T was way ahead of its time.

Ford mastered the art of refining requirements to meet the customer's unspoken wants and needs and then fulfilling them with the most cost-effective design available. Although there were other cars in the marketplace, none could compete with Ford's Model T in features, efficiency, and affordability. Ford had mastered the art of developing his product based on clear and concise objective statements.

In the innovative lean development culture, teams are encouraged to create a clearly defined set of problem statements at the start of each discovery step to ensure that the learning cycles are successful. Within the learning cycles, the learning objectives are expanded by listing specific questions that further document what is not known about solving the problem. A cascading path is created from the objective to the specific questions that need to be asked, and then to the tasks that need to be done to answer the question.

A team used this approach to modify a wall-mounted computer station to allow the support column to mount to the side, allowing the unit to slide up and down. This is the objective. To do this, the team needed to move the support column from the center of the unit to the side to allow the computer to mount parallel to the wall with minimal encroachment on the knee space. Figure 3.6 illustrates the process and shows how the objective cascades down through questions and tasks. The objectives, questions, and tasks are developed in the first days of the planning phase of the learning cycle. The team then rounds out all of the tasks that need to be completed, and they

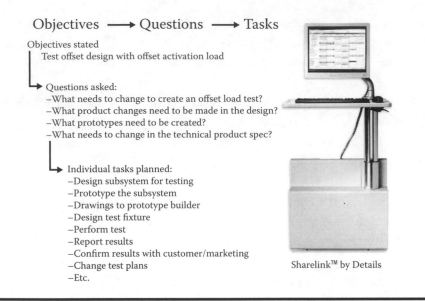

Objectives ⟶ Questions ⟶ Tasks

Objectives stated
  Test offset design with offset activation load

Questions asked:
  –What needs to change to create an offset load test?
  –What product changes need to be made in the design?
  –What prototypes need to be created?
  –What needs to change in the technical product spec?

Individual tasks planned:
  –Design subsystem for testing
  –Prototype the subsystem
  –Drawings to prototype builder
  –Design test fixture
  –Perform test
  –Report results
  –Confirm results with customer/marketing
  –Change test plans
  –Etc.

Sharelink™ by Details

Figure 3.6 Learning cycle objectives expanded with questions and tasks.

become part of the team accountability board and are managed visually to ensure that the pace of development is maintained.

How to Keep Options Open with Multiple Concepts

Learning cycles are done in rapid iterations to accelerate learning. Iterations occur daily, so that learning continues constantly. The parts or ideas evolve and improve over time to meet more and more of the customer wants and create less and less waste in the process.

In lean set-based development, multiple concepts are considered simultaneously to solve a problem. As development progresses, it is common for several solutions to be proposed at various times. All too often, however, the team grabs hold of the solution that seems best to them and then runs with it as far as possible. Often the solution is optimized even though it has obvious flaws, which results in waste when that flawed solution is later eliminated, and there are no other backup solutions.

That is a very large waste because the team must now reevaluate the previous options, try another or next best option, and repeat the process. This requires tremendous rework. Because it is common for this scenario to be repeated for several concepts, the project team must scramble to adjust the schedule, the costs, the performance, and finally the expectations of management and customers.

The classic lean wastes can be restated and defined for the development process:

Waiting	= interdependent people, handoffs
Inventory	= limited reuse of designs
Overproduction	= unused bells and whistles
Overprocessing	= completing concepts that are discarded
Defects	= rework late in the project (or in the field!)
Excess motion	= ineffective communication
Non-value-added processing	= point-based solutions pursued too long

To these we can add another waste:

Underutilized people	= discarded or lost knowledge

While some may seem to overlap, focus for a moment on the wastes that occur because a decision is made too early. Perhaps the most obvious is the REWORK waste. When we develop a solution far down the path, only to see it discarded for some reason, we need a ready backup. For this reason, in innovative lean development, carrying multiple solutions forward is important. The idea is to carry as many ideas along as possible until you must eliminate them, keeping a strong stable of solutions in your development plan.

Think of this in terms of a development schedule and aim to delay the design freeze as long as possible. This gives the team a chance to recover when things don't go as planned (actually, we all know we need to plan for things that will not go as planned).

Based on the given end date in the block plan, the team can develop the milestone for flawless execution, or no rework. That is the design freeze. Up to that design freeze, the development team should continue to learn about all solution options, so that it won't be caught without a solution.

There is a trade-off for carrying these forward—discarding completed concepts is one of the lean wastes. The alternative, however, is unacceptable. In the Toyota production system, this is known as the Toyota paradox. By carrying multiple concepts forward, more time will be spent in the early concept and development stages. With the design freeze at a true flawless execution point, however, the implementation phase is much faster (and less expensive) than traditional development, delivering the product in less time overall. Look again at Figure 3.2. It illustrates how delaying the design freeze as long as possible, closing all design gaps and issues, shortens the execution phase.

By keeping more concepts going until the team must decide on one, the team eliminates the need for vast amounts of rework—the project schedule killer. Keeping multiple concepts alive can also benefit the team as it plays these concepts against each other along the way. This evolving and improving design also maximizes product quality, a clear customer want.

> *Minimizing waste and maximizing customer values*
> *are part of innovative lean development.*

How to Use Extensive Checklists

There are many ideas about how to make product development a lean development system. Visual controls are a key technique to ensure pace is maintained and that tasks are completed. However, other things also need to be tracked; for example, how do we ensure we are working on the right things; how does the team know if it is missing anything; are the other project tasks being completed on time?

The team needs a way to merge its new lean development techniques with the wisdom found in traditional phase gate processes. Even though the phase gate process might be slow and inefficient, it is great for keeping track of all the tiny details that might otherwise get lost during development. For this reason, it is important to merge the learning cycle approach into the existing approach.

Whether the team decides to maintain the existing phase gate method or revamp it completely is not as important as making sure its key techniques are put into practice. An extreme makeover is not necessary as long as the important tasks are accounted for in the new combined process. This means that in addition to tracking the tasks at the detail level, the team's development knowledge also must be captured. To do this, checklists and standards are still needed. Teams need to combine the "what needs to be done" checklists and standards with the "maintain the pace of what needs to be done" process of visual controls. Project tasks should be separated from innovation and learning tasks by using one color for the project tasks and another for the innovation and learning tasks so they stand out. Making them visual enhances communication, and tracking them ensures that they are done.

As development progresses, look for opportunities to define what completeness looks like. Too many projects stumble because teams only have a vague notion of what a completed step really looks like. If there is no definition of what key endpoints look like, the team can't know if the goal has been achieved. If any project goal is undefined, use a template or checklist to define what the completed goal should look like. If the team has a clear goal, it is more likely to get there.

Defining completed project goals will remove several key wastes, among them, the excess motion resulting from poor communication. Capturing checklists will avoid losing knowledge for the next team and the next project. Table 3.1 lists some common problems and the types of checklists that might be needed to solve them.

Table 3.1   Common Development Problems and Potential Solutions

Common Problem	*Checklist and Standards*
Unclear project objectives at the start	Checklist defining a statement of the true need
Definition of what "pass" and "fail" is for this product	Test standards and test requirements
Definition of what is needed to integrate this component into the system and to make it compatible with other products in the portfolio	Checklist of common interface steps and what needs to be considered for compatibility
Process for selecting and distinguishing among the leading concepts	Define key attributes and measure the concepts using spider charts (see Chapter 6)
Definition of profitability for this product	Checklists and templates to meet accounting needs
Determining when the design is complete and the true design freeze point	A list of required tasks and design steps
Establishing when the product will come to market and when the IT system can accommodate it	Complete readiness checklist to ensure that the important steps are covered

These are just a few examples. The important thing is to capture them in the development process by including these checklists and templates in the process. Fulfilling the requirements of a checklist and templates is a lot more effective than living with the unknown and uncomfortable feeling that something is missing. Finally, to ensure that the checklists and templates are created in a timely fashion, make the completion of the checklists and templates a part of the learning cycles by managing them visually.

How to Design a Timeline

An important step is to define the timeline for each project in detail. The concept of learning cycles can be applied to any large project, which can be broken down into the multiple learning cycles needed to answer the learning objectives. The number of learning cycles is determined by tallying the number of objectives. The sequence of learning objectives needs to be considered. Some objectives must precede others. Another consideration is the timeline available in which to develop the solution. By setting the number and duration of learning cycles, a solid block plan is developed.

How to Tie Multiple Teams Together with Integration Events

The final step of a learning cycle is sharing the knowledge gained in an integration event, where the teams review the results of the learning cycle. To ensure parallel teams work to the same schedule, the leader should schedule the date of the integration event before the individual teams are scheduled to put their pieces together in one composite, combined build. This has worked with a large system level project with as many as eight major subteams, all working in parallel.

Each team works at its own pace, some completing more learning cycles than others do between the integration events. However, all the teams focus on the integration event to bring their individual parts together. The teams should never allow the date for the integration event to slip. The event is a key project milestone.

Integration events include:

■ Documenting the key knowledge gained
■ Focusing on completing the objectives of the learning cycle

- Comparing desired to actual project schedule
- Mapping out the next learning cycle
- Planning and requesting resources for the next cycle

The integration event gives project leadership the opportunity to tie things together across the teams for overall project updates and go-forward planning. This event is the structured touch point for management involvement in the project. It is a time to evaluate, to ask, "Where are we? Are we there yet? How do we get there?" The idea is to integrate the people, ideas, goals, and schedule at the same time. It is a snapshot of how the project is doing and gives management the opportunity to exercise its responsibility to steer the project in the best direction.

The integration event, as the structured touch point, gives management the occasion to ask a set of questions that keep projects on track. The four that follow are a good place to begin:

1. *What has the team learned?* This question puts the focus squarely on learning—where it belongs—rather than on team activity. Leadership should be driving the team to learn.
2. *How does the short-term schedule look?* The team needs focus on the short term to be sure the project stays on track. The next milestone or event is a good focus. A regular pitch at integration events gives the team and management a better chance at success.
3. *How does the long-term schedule look?* Of course, the project must finish on time. Integration events, with all the team members and the management team present, are perfect settings to discuss the overall schedule.
4. *What general issues does the team have?* The first three questions are more general and apply to the overall strategy of the organization. This one is specific to the things that need to be addressed immediately, including flow interrupters and issues that require management attention.

The learning cycle and integration event schedule in Figure 3.7 looks very tidy. We all know that in real projects, a block plan schedule looks more like Figure 3.8. The subsystem development teams still have integration events after each learning cycle, but the full system build, integrating the results of multiple learning cycles from each subteam, is forced to occur at an intermediate checkpoint.

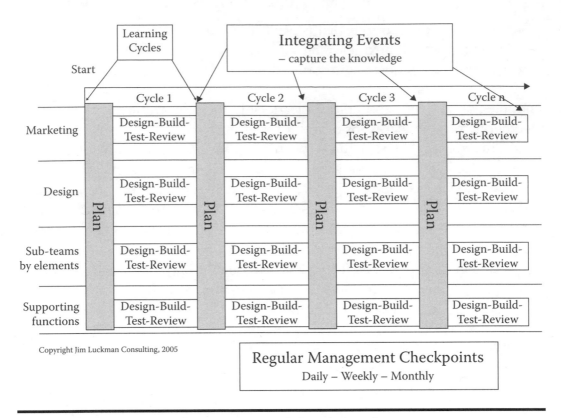

Figure 3.7   Integration events close out each learning cycle.

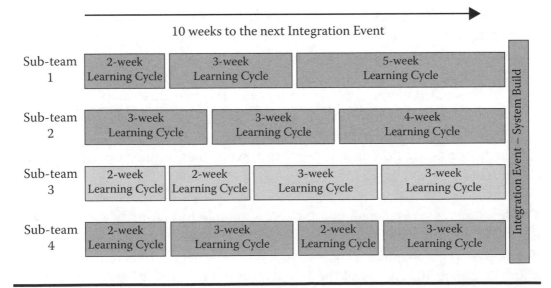

Figure 3.8   Integration event: parallel learning cycles vary in pitch but come together in the integration event.

Table 3.2   Integration Event Standard Work and Meeting Agenda

Integration Event Standard Work and Meeting Agenda
Agenda: Review this learning cycle's objectives as outlined in the scope document. Review the highlights from the integration checklist for the learning cycle (red: missed item, or out of tolerance; green: satisfied requirements). Address any flow interrupters that arose during the last learning cycle. Review the objective summary statements and percent complete and accurate. Review the team recommendations for the next learning cycle. Outline the next learning cycle, including high-level objectives, budget, resources, and timing.

To do before Integration Event (project leader)
 	
Integration checklist:
 	
    Answer the questions in the checklist.
    Mark the items with a red or green dot.
    Strike through any items that do not apply.
    Scope document questions for this learning cycle.
    Make sure each question has an answer.
    Create bullet points in objective summary.
 	
State the percent complete and an accurate estimate for each objective (can be based on the number of questions with complete answers out of the total number of questions for that objective).

Summary section Complete the team recommendation (after soliciting feedback and opinions from the team in the team meetings). Outline the next learning cycle (use the last learning cycle's team meeting(s) for this task). Present the high-level objectives, and pull in "future questions" from the current learning cycle (team discussions during the integration event will set the direction as well as questions for the next learning cycle).
To do after the Integration Event (project leader) Build the scope document for the next learning cycle. Complete the objectives. Define all questions that should be answered by the team during the next learning cycle for each objective. Create the next daily accountability board with the team adding its tasks. Capture the knowledge gained.

The primary focus of the integration event is on the build and what was learned about it as the product was assembled rather than on the project details. The teams present a brief project overview of key issues, cost targets, and a summary of what has been learned. The integration event is another opportunity to capture new issues exposed and to record the knowledge gained by the teams.

A typical integration event agenda might look like Table 3.2.

Keep the integration event tight and concise. The presentation should be minimal; the focus is on how things work together. A standard format, along with practice, will keep these meetings valuable.

Chapter 4

How to Optimize Problem Solving Using Multiple Learning Cycles

"The most serious mistakes are not being made as a result of wrong answers. The truly dangerous thing is asking the wrong questions."

Peter Drucker, *Men, Ideas & Politics*

Learning cycles lead to optimized solutions. For rapid development to be successful, implement lean learning cycles and religiously adhere to deadlines.

Project leaders use learning cycles to increase speed, give direction, gain continuous feedback and adjustment, and foster a learning culture. To optimize learning, a cross-team plan must be developed for all resources. Remember, the goal is speed, so approve all of the resources as much as possible in advance. As we have seen, the beauty of learning cycles is the short time frame, which is a tremendous advantage in business, because there is a focus and increased knowledge of what can be achieved in these 3 to 4 weeks. Teams can maximize this advantage by avoiding wasted time; for example, by approving learning cycle spending ahead of time, increasing spending authorization in advance of the learning cycle, and working to anticipate hurdles in support of speed. Estimating resources and spending becomes less difficult with the smaller windows of time found in learning cycles.

Tying things and people together quickly often embodies many of the lean principles necessary for innovative lean development. This practice helps fill the team's knowledge gaps and promotes learning as the goal of development. Learning cycles are the short bursts of learning to help develop speed, but they must be structured to properly define the problems to work on, and iteration must happen rapidly.

Overall, the goal of learning cycles is to develop a learning organization, give and receive feedback in order to adjust the project, monitor the project direction, and increase development and innovation speed. All this will likely require a cultural shift in most organizations. Successful participation starts and ends with management involvement. Seek out and engage leadership that will help the effort. Cultivate a cadre of believers. Start small if you must, but start.

Case Study: Typical Learning Cycle

Development bursts, these learning cycles, have a scheduling component that fits into the organization's development plan, but how does it work? Learning cycles have structure and discipline, but what do they look like?

Some of the things product development is concerned with are structure, aesthetics, and cost. As a rule, trade-offs among these and many other things must be evaluated to satisfy customer needs and company requirements. If the discussion can be framed around how some factors affect others, then team members can learn and make educated choices using better information.

Take a simple example: the junction between the vertical leg of a table and its horizontal foot. Now consider the large number of options that must be evaluated with regard to aesthetics, structure, and cost in this area alone. After examining all of the foot options, all the leg options, and the resulting combinations, the challenge is to evaluate and choose solutions that satisfy customer needs, company design criteria, industry performance standards, and financial targets. The trade-off between aesthetic choices and their cost is a key design factor; therefore, it becomes a learning cycle objective.

In learning cycles, objectives drive questions, and questions drive tasks for the accountability board. Continuing with this example, the questions that needed answering are:

- Of the possible leg and foot solutions, what are the aesthetically allowable leg/foot combinations?
- What is the allowable cost for the combinations?
- How does aesthetics impact cost?

To answer these questions, tasks must be assigned to team members, who will chase down answers. For the first question, the tasks are to:

- Identify all the leg possibilities
- Identify all the foot possibilities
- Identify all leg/foot combinations
- Evaluate the combinations

For the second question:

- Develop the costs of all combinations
- Evaluate (with design) the aesthetics of each option

For the last question:

- Show the trade-offs of cost versus aesthetics

In a summary format, this learning cycle might look like Figure 4.1.

Couple this with an accountability board (see Figure 4.2) for task management and team member assignments and the learning cycle is underway. Remember, these learning cycles should be short—2 to 4 weeks—in duration.

The output of a learning cycle includes the knowledge gained, preferably in a trade-off format. In this example, a concept comparison grid is created (see Figure 4.3), and the results are transferred to a trade-off curve for knowledge capture (see Figure 4.4).

Controlled Release of Work

Even a very efficient development methodology such as learning cycles can be overburdened by too many projects. Usually, the demands on the development organization are more than the staff can handle. This is true in both product development and IT development. The competition must be

Learning Cycle Goals/Deliverables (Objectives)
What will be accomplished during this learning cycle?
The focus of this learning cycle is to achieve the following business goals:

Objective 1:   Compare the aesthetics of the leg/foot solutions with the costs
Objective 2:   [Most learning cycles will have multiple objectives]
Objective 3:

Questions to answer in this learning cycle:

1. Objective 1
    1.1. Question 1: Of the possible leg and foot solutions, what are the aesthetically allowable leg/foot combinations?
        1.1.1.   Task 1.1: Identify all the leg possibilities – Debbie
        1.1.2.   Task 1.2: Identify all the foot possibilities – Debbie
        1.1.3.   Task 1.3: Identify all leg/foot combinations – Steve
        1.1.4.   Task 1.4: Evaluate the combinations – Jon
    1.2. Question 2: What is the allowable cost for each combination?
        1.2.1.   Task 2.1: Develop all combination costs – Becca
        1.2.2.   Task 2.2: Evaluate with design for aesthetics – David
    1.3. Question 3: How do aesthetics impact cost?
        1.3.1.   Task 3.1: Show the trade-offs for costs v. aesthetics – Jon

2. Objective 2
    2.1. Question 1:
    2.2. Question 2:

3. Objective 3
    3.1. Question 1:
    3.2. Question 2:

4. Other Questions
    4.1. Question 1:
    4.2. Question 2:

Figure 4.1   Learning cycle task list and team member assignments.

answered when they release their latest product, which will soon make all others obsolete, and the organization's demand for the next technology solution always needs to be met as soon as possible.

A well-established lean manufacturing principle is that large batch requests without focus quickly lead to inefficiencies, excess inventory, and rework. Similarly, the development process will quickly bog down if it

Project: Better Table
Learning cycle #4
Daily activity plan
Last updated: October 3

Week of:	Monday 10/6 *(15–30 minute team update meeting)*	Tuesday 10/7	Wednesday 10/8 *(15–30 minute team update meeting)*	Thursday 10/9	Friday 10/10	Monday 10/13 *(15–30 minute team update meeting)*	Tuesday 10/14	Wednesday 10/15 *(15–30 minute team update meeting)*	Thursday 10/16	Friday 10/17
Debbie (Engineering)	●◎ Identify all leg possibilities		◎ Identify all foot possibilities		◎ Identify all leg/foot combinations	◎ Evaluate all leg/foot combinations				
Steve (Marketing)					◎ Identify all leg/foot combinations	●◎ Evaluate all leg/foot combinations		◎ Evaluate all leg/foot combinations for aesthetics	◎ Show cost v. aesthetics trade-offs	INTEGRATION EVENT 10:00 am
Becca (Supply Chain)						◎ Evaluate all leg/foot combinations		◎ Evaluate all leg/foot combination costs		
Jon (Project Management)						◎ Evaluate all leg/foot combinations			◎ Show cost v. aesthetics trade-offs	
Laura (Supplier)						◎ Evaluate all leg/foot combinations		◎ Develop all leg/foot combination costs		
David (Industrial Design)						●◎ Evaluate all leg/foot combinations		◎ Evaluate all leg/foot combinations for aesthetics		
Legend:	Complete = ◎		Not Complete = ●							

Figure 4.2 Accountability board for a learning cycle.

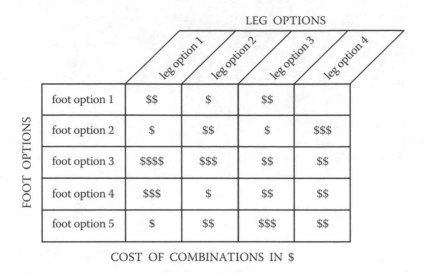

Figure 4.3   **A concept comparison grid of a single dimension of the design.**

receives too many requests at the same time. When too many parallel tasks are attempted, something will suffer.

In manufacturing, the need to build multiple products simultaneously demands a careful design of the process: the line must be balanced to handle multiple products using the principles of load leveling and mixed model

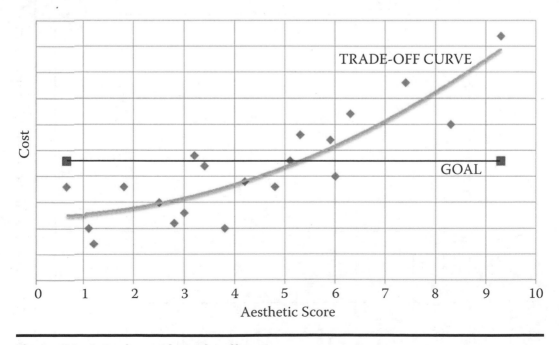

Figure 4.4   **Learning cycle trade-off curve.**

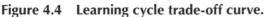

production. The line must be carefully analyzed and timed to determine which products can be made in the same process. If three models are to be built, say model A, B, and C, each with different work content, the correct combination for building the models must be designed into the process. If the degree of difficulty ranges from low (model A), to medium (model B), to high (model C), then the mix must be carefully arranged (see Figure 4.5). For example, all of the easy models should not be built in the morning leaving the complex ones to be built late in the day because that would not give the workers time to recover should they run into trouble in the afternoon. In addition, if customer demand is mixed across the three models, the lean value stream manufacturing line should build some of each throughout the day. Furthermore, it is easier and ergonomically desirable for the workers to build different models throughout the day.

The need in the manufacturing process is to balance out the takt time, or pace, at every station in the process. To do this, the sequence must be correct and work must be released based on what the production line is designed to build.

Similarly, in development the capacity of the team is often split into large, medium, and small projects as well as life cycle maintenance (LCM) requests. The capacity of the team or individual can be determined, and the amount of work that can be assigned at any given time can be carefully released in order not to overload the workers (see Figure 4.6).

The best way to manage the release of work into a development group is by using a visual control board. Unassigned projects are listed on one side of the board; teams are listed in another. The current team (or individual) workloads along with the current assignments are listed in another section of the board. As teams complete projects, new work can be assigned from the unassigned projects list (see Figure 4.7).

Controlled Release of Work in Manufacturing
If the demand per shift is for: • 4 Model "A" (most complex) • 6 Model "B" (moderately complex) • 16 Model "C" (least complex)
Then the mixed model production schedule will be: C C A C C B B C C A C C B B C C A C C B B C C A C C

Figure 4.5   Sample of a controlled-release manufacturing schedule.

Controlled Release of Work in Development
If the capacity of the development team (or individual) is determined to be:
• Large project "L": 16 hours per week. Large projects always span more than 1 week to complete. • Medium projects "M": 8 hours per week. Projects taking an average of 4 hours to complete. • Small project "S": 6 hours per week. Projects taking an average of 2 hours to complete. • Life cycle maintenance (LCM) projects: 6 hours per week. LCM projects take an average of 2 hours to complete. • Process improvement and administrative tasks: 4 hours per week.
The remaining projects to work on in a given week are based on demand and are determined by the team or its leadership.   Sample workload for one 40-hour week: two small projects (4 hours), one medium project (4 hours), large project (16 hours), one small project (2 hours), one medium (4 hours), and three LCM projects (6 hours). (Note: 4 hours are unaccounted for because the employee will have other responsibilities, such as team meetings. Generally, the worker is never loaded to 100% of available time.)

Figure 4.6   Sample controlled release development schedule.

Weekly Controlled Release of Work Development Projects
Unassigned Projects
Large projects   L5 (w/description)   L6 (w/description)

Medium projects   M19 (w/description)
                              M20 (w/description)
                              M21 (w/description)

Small projects   S127
                        S128
                        S129

Life Cycle Management Projects   LCM189
                                                    LCM190
                                                    LCM191

Team 1 Assignments L2, M12, M15, S120, S122, S123, LCM182, LCM185, LCM Open
Team 2 Assignments L4, M11, M16, M18, S Open, S119, S124, LCM181, LCM183, LCM184
Team 3 Assignments L3, M13, M17, S121, S125, S126, LCM186, LCM187, LCM188

Figure 4.7   Sample visual board for controlled release of projects for development.

The visual control board performs several functions for both the leadership and the teams:

- At any given time, who is working on each project is known.
- Unassigned projects are immediately visible.
- As the teams complete assignments, the capacity is known.

In Figure 4.7, team 1 has capacity for an LCM project, and team 2 has capacity for a small project but is overloaded by one medium project. They should be assigned only two medium projects and three small projects, but actually have three medium projects and two small ones. The reasons for the exceptions would be discussed during a team meeting.

Visual control boards are always referred to during the team standup meetings, which should meet at regular intervals to review the project assignments. If the board is a weekly board, then meeting on a pitch of twice a week should be sufficient to keep track of changes in the assignments.

Any number of refinements could be made to the board. For example,

- The prioritization of incoming projects could be indicated visually.
- Assignments of projects could be made in between the meetings using a standard week.
- Completed projects could be included.
- Projected end dates for projects could be included, and the status of projects could be noted: red if late and green if on time.

By posting expected completion dates, the team and the leaders could stage work to be started as soon as team capacity is freed up. The reason a project is late can also be shown on the board and discussed by the team. Process improvement suggestions and ideas might also be included.

Any customization of the board should be done with the team, so that the team develops ownership to meet the needs in the organization. The capacity and assignment process will have to be revised once a track record is established for completing lean development projects.

How to Use the Learning Cycle Scope Document

Since development is both heuristic and focused on delivering a solution, some attention must be given to the task-oriented project activities required to implement the system and the discoveries and innovation that must occur. In other words, every single learning cycle can account for both task-driven events (such as meeting key project deliverables) as well as learning objectives.

The governing document for the learning cycles is the learning cycle scope document, and it should account for both the discoveries needed to achieve the objective and the key implementation tasks required. This process is repeated through each phase of the project. The implementation deliverables become the general objectives of the learning cycle, and the discoveries that must be made become learning objectives. The learning cycle scope document is a guide to structuring the learning cycles.

The elements of the scope document include the following:

Learning Cycle n

This label identifies the learning cycle. Since learning cycles are usually sequential, they can be labeled with a number. However, in some cases parallel teams may be performing concurrent learning cycles on different elements of the system (subsystems). In the case of multiple parallel learning cycles, the name of the subsystem can be used to identify the learning cycles. For example, if there were three parallel teams—one for the network, one for the servers, and one for the software—each would be identified, and each would have its own number: Network Learning Cycle 3, Server Learning Cycle 3, and Software Learning Cycle 4, and so on. The learning cycles are tracked on the block plan schedule, and all of the subteam learning cycles are listed on the block plan.

Learning Cycle Goals/Deliverables (Objectives)

In this section of the scope document, the team lists the project deliverables and the learning objectives. The team will want to tie in the specific things that must be done with the phase gate implementation plan by listing them in this section. The learning cycles are intended to support the higher-level deliverables, and, by listing them in this section, the team can stay focused on what it needs to do during the learning cycle that is before them.

Learning Cycle Scope Document

Learning Cycle Number: _____

Learning Cycle Goals/Deliverables (Objectives): What will be accomplished in this learning cycle?

1. Goal/Deliverable 1 (Owner)
2. Goal/Deliverable 2 (Owner)
3. Goal/Deliverable 3 (Owner)

Learning Objectives and Questions to Answer:

Learning Objective 1:
1. Question 1.1 (Owner)
2. Question 1.2 (Owner)
3. Question 1.3 (Owner)

Learning Objective 2:
1. Question 2.1 (Owner)
2. Question 2.2 (Owner)
3. Question 2.3 (Owner)

Measures and Project Management Structure

1. Measurement 1
2. Measurement 2
3. Measurement 3

Outside Resource Requirements

1. Resource 1 xx%
2. Resource 2 xx%
3. Resource 3 xx%

1. Prototype Costs $xx
2. Contractor Costs $xx

Things to be documented at the end of the learning cycle:

Key Knowledge Gained
• Lesson 1
• Lesson 2
• Lesson 3

Issues to review with stakeholders (to gain input and direction):
1. Issue 1
2. Issue 2
3. Issue 3

Team Recommendation/Conclusion for Learning Cycle:

Figure 4.8   A learning cycle scope document for a single cycle.

For example, information technology requires a mixture of learning cycles and specific task-oriented items. These are split into two distinct items to manage the project: the learning cycle scope document is used to discover and answer questions (the process of discovery) and the IT checklist tasks to fulfill project deliverables. The learning cycle scope document is used to manage the major learning objectives and questions that need to be answered. The scope document describes the specific items that must be learned and what questions must be answered to meet those objectives. As the questions are answered, the responses are stored in the scope document.

Tasks that need to be accomplished for the project deliverables come from checklists, as Figure 4.9 shows.

IT Checklists
Update issues list
Create master test plan
Determine how to test
Identify unit & integration test scenarios
Set up environment
Validate data
Validate testing tools
Validate test reports for functionality
Contact other teams for status of their construction progress
Create training materials & plans in project folder
Create program documentation
Create appropriate security access rights
Contact teams sending data to you
Contact teams receiving data from you
Create design specifications from template in subfolder
Review & update this checklist with tollgate team

Figure 4.9 Sample IT checklist to use during development.

This checklist is not exhaustive, but represents some of the things that need to be accounted for in every IT project. The purpose of checklists is to remind the team of the best-in-class techniques that should be used on every project. The activities listed are in addition to the learning cycles not in place of them. We recommend that these same items appear on the visual accountability board in a different color than learning cycle items.

The owner of each deliverable is listed behind the objective. Ownership is a key element because it allows the team to track the item on the accountability board by the person who owns the deliverable. To help separate the project deliverables from the learning objectives, the two different types of objectives are assigned a specific color on the visual control board (blue might be used for project deliverables and yellow for learning objectives). All of the tasks associated with each objective should be posted on the visual control board; they should follow the color scheme used for the objectives to indicate that they belong to either a project deliverable or a learning objective. It is also important to maintain a unique numbering scheme for each objective and task, which should be linked to the objectives.

Learning Objectives and Questions

In this section, the specific questions needing answers for this cycle's objectives are listed. The questions represent the project's true unknowns (these could be technical problems, software configuration problems, or even methods). Often there are several methods that a team could use to accomplish the results; usually, there are trade-offs between the methods. One method might be easier to implement but harder to support later on. Another method might have the best user interface but might require more programming time to implement. Each of these can become a learning cycle objective. In the example just cited, the learning objective and questions might be:

- *Learning Objective 1:* **Document the trade-offs between programming effort and the ease of use of the user interface for options A, B, and C.**
  Question 1.1: What modules need to be customized and programmed to achieve the ease of use for the user?
  Question 1.2: What effort will be required for each customized module for options A, B, and C?

Question 1.3: Based on simple visual prototypes, what module designs are easiest to use?

Framing the learning objectives carefully for each learning cycle will lead to the study of the unknown. Usually, once the team frames the initial objectives and questions, other questions and unknowns are quickly uncovered. These will either fit into the current learning cycle or have to be delayed and saved for a future learning cycle.

The project manager's role is to track the process, making sure that the correct objectives and questions are included in the current learning cycle, and then to ensure that the scope of the current learning cycle does not grow by recording objectives and questions to be included in the next learning cycle.

Measures and Project Management Structure

In this section of the scope document, the team records the things it is trying to achieve. These often focus on time, quality, and cost—for example, the length of the current learning cycle, the expected performance of the system and test criteria for acceptance, and what the team expects to spend in order to meet the goals.

All prototypes should be listed in this section. If the team expects to build a prototype of the computing server environment, that activity should be documented along with any other types of prototypes.

Outside Resource Requirements

- Resource 1 xx% (percentage of availability of time for this team member on this learning cycle)
- Resource 2 xx%
- Resource 3 xx%
- Prototype costs $xx for this learning cycle
- Contractor costs $xx for this learning cycle

It may be tempting to overlook this section; however, identifying the inside and outside resources (contractors or consultants) required and what percentage of time the team members are able to devote to each during the learning cycle allows the project leadership to evaluate the need in terms of cost and time.

The benefits are tremendous. Not only is the need for the required resources very clear, the resources of the entire team are made very explicit. Having explicit resources named for each short learning cycle allows each resource to clearly understand its role and allows it to focus the appropriate amount of time and energy to the project. Because a learning cycle is typically no more than 30 days long, the resource assignments for a specific length of time are known. This brings an entirely new focus to the planning process. Resources can be devoted to the learning cycle, yet the resource model remains flexible. Furthermore, if the project manager uses a visual planning board with accountability stickers, then the manager will know down to the week and even the day when a resource is needed or when the resource can be released for other work on another project.

In this section, the prototype costs are also estimated and listed. This is not a substitute for the overall budget and estimated costs. Certainly, the project will still need to be justified to management. What is different is that by listing the learning cycle budget for prototypes, an accurate projection of the cost of the next learning cycle can be shared.

More important, by indicating the cost prior to the start of the learning cycle, the team is asking for agreement on how much they will need to spend before work begins. This is a key step because the team can estimate clearly what needs to be done in the next learning cycle and how much will need to be spent, but it can rarely estimate accurately beyond that point. In addition, having preapproval to spend money and use the proper resources for the next cycle increases the speed of execution because a potential flow interrupter has been removed from the next learning cycle before it has a chance to surface.

Key Knowledge Gained

- Lesson 1
- Lesson 2
- Lesson 3

The key things learned are captured at the end of the learning cycle, and they are recorded in the scope document for presentation to the leadership of the team. Usually, these are formally presented to management at the integration event. Remember to schedule the integration event at the beginning of the learning cycle so that everyone knows the end date, and plans for it in their schedule. No one should be surprised at the end of the learning cycle that an integration event is about to occur.

When the team records all knowledge gained, it is capturing a summary of the objectives and questions answered. Additionally, as it moves through the learning cycle, the team should be recording the answers to all the specific questions that were listed earlier in the learning cycle.

This section provides a summary of all knowledge that can be shared with the whole team and management. The entire team may not be aware of the activities and learning of each subteam, so the key knowledge gained by each subteam should be shared with all team members and stakeholders. Discussion around the learning cycles will allow the whole team to reflect on the last learning cycle and prepare for the next.

Issues and Flow Interrupters

- Issue 1
- Issue 2
- Issue 3

Similarly, any key issues or flow interrupters that occurred during the learning cycle are shared with the leadership team. The issues listed in the scope document should be only the ones affecting the team, summarized from the issues lists that are usually maintained elsewhere by the team in a spreadsheet or database. In this section, only the issues that still need the attention of leadership should appear.

Team Recommendations/Conclusion for Learning Cycle

Finally, the team shares its conclusions and makes recommendations for what should occur in the next learning cycle. This gives the project manager and the leadership a glimpse into the next learning cycle. It is highly recommended that the team prepare an initial draft of the scope document for the next learning cycle to share with the leadership at the integration event. In this way, the team can discuss the specific objectives as well as share thoughts on what resources (both time and financial commitments) will be required for the next cycle.

Chapter 5

How to Use Value Stream Mapping to Stabilize, Measure, and Control the Learning Process

"A bad system will beat a good person every time."

W. Edwards Deming, professor, author, lean consultant

Lean has been called a cost-cutting system, but that is not entirely accurate. Lean is an *improvement* system. To improve, we must search for problems and work to eliminate their causes, even when no problems seem to exist.

How to Stabilize the Process

To do this, lean thinkers need to understand their process to drive the desired improvement; however, before they can do this, the process needs to be stable, in order to establish a base for change. Business is after results, but the process is what delivers those results. An unstable process is an unproductive process. All of the gears of the process have to be aligned and oiled for the machine of development to run smoothly. If they are not, even the greatest heroics cannot make the machine run.

Toyota uses the chief engineer to pull together the various aspects of the development process. The chief engineer must not only run the technical areas of the project, but also make key marketing and design decisions. This is a daunting task.

While the idea of a chief engineer in lean development might seem desirable, the practicality of giving all of the decision-making authority to one person is questionable. Furthermore, many people note that it does not fit with American business culture. An alternative approach is to work on two different elements. First, work should be done on the process, stabilizing it and measuring it to ensure that it is running like the well-oiled machine it should be. This will take some of the pressure off the organization and the individuals in it. Second, the topic of governance needs to be addressed. When the machine exhibits problems and needs to be fixed, or when decisions need to be made, or when team conflicts and problems need to be addressed, a group of leaders must be ready to jump in and make the needed decisions.

Measure Ideas in Order to Learn

Measuring is something the corporate world does all the time. Financial analysts measure how we performed last quarter. Executives measure how the performance did against the plan. Business experts measure how the company performed compared to its competitors. Stockholders measure the company's performance with respect to the previous year, and they watch how the stock market analysts perceive their company. These are typical and perhaps worthy measures, but notice how all these measurements look backward. Innovation needs real-time measurements that are forward facing in order to be worthwhile.

An innovator who is developing a new solution is always working toward the future, toward the target. The measurements most useful for innovation require that we determine how we are doing against that target in real time. If you were driving from Chicago to Boston and the route was new to you, you would occasionally check your compass, map, or even your global positioning system to see if you were going in the right direction. If you had taken a wrong turn, a quick check of the map would give you the feedback required to correct course and continue toward the target. Similarly, in development, it is the adjustments we make now that are crucial to ensure we hit the target at the end of the project.

Predictive measures are the measurements that we do to learn.* This is precisely the goal for measuring during an innovative lean development process.

The purpose of measuring is to learn.

When new ideas are measured against customer values (defined by the customer wants), and when new ideas are measured against the wastes to avoid, they can be minimized. The act of measuring against the stated values and wastes is a clear connection to the goals of the project, the end-in-view.

What gets measured gets done. Furthermore, what gets measured can be understood. Measurement helps make corrections rational, and shows where opportunities exist. The task of process improvement on the learning process typically is assigned to process leaders in an organization and is carried out by the lean champion or expert (sometimes called a lean black belt) in the organization. The lean champion will optimize the design by measuring how well the team moves toward its targets in real time, always looking forward. This will keep the connection to the project goals clear and will help your project make the innovation leap.

Innovation fills the gaps between here and there; measuring to learn is the only way to know if you are accomplishing this.

By measuring solutions, we can compare where we started or where we are against where we are going. This helps teams understand how we arrived and where we want to go. To do this, design measures to identify gaps. If you know where the gaps are between where you want to go and where you are, you stand a much better chance of reducing that gap. The team must be vigilant in finding the gaps and relentless in reducing them; that is when it will make the jump in innovation. To do this:

■ The team must be involved in creating the measures. Their ownership of the measurement is required, as this will drive commitment. The project will start out with given goals, but the team can develop the measures that will demonstrate how well the solution accomplishes those goals.

---

* Bart Huthwaite. *The Rules of Innovation*, p. 111.

- Determine what problems need to be solved; these are the initial gaps to be addressed.
- Once measures are agreed upon at the team level, management approval is needed to support the measures that will produce the desired results.
- Progress is measured at regular intervals along the product development road. How often measures are checked depends on how long the team can afford to wait before a correction may be needed (in lean terms, this is called *pitch*, see Chapter 3).

To determine which ideas are the best ideas, it is important to remember what the team is trying to accomplish. To do this the team must always keep the end in view. By working backward from that target, the innovator will always maintain a clear connection to the values of the customer. Measuring new ideas against these values and ideas against the wastes leads to an optimized design. Innovation requires effective measurement.

How to Measure the Process

The customer evaluates a company's products or services using time, cost, and quality measures. This is also how companies should measure themselves. These are measures of results, but they are really also measures of process.

The lean expert should look at the company's organization chart to determine if there is a discernable process (processes are horizontal paths, across multiple functional areas). None will be seen unless the organization is already highly process oriented. Organizations do not typically think, plan, work, count, organize, or manage this way. The focus is on function. Yet the customers are concerned with the output of the entire end-to-end process, stretching from the beginning to the end of all the business activities required for the process to function (also known as the *value stream*).

Think of an end-to-end process. Does the process cross functional boundaries, but remain organized by functional management silos? How does management measure each function? What are the measures? Are the measures process oriented, or merely there to measure the effectiveness of the functional silo? The measures are almost always some version of time, cost, and quality.

The same process that measures customers' experience when interacting with a company also connect cross-functionally across the process. Thus, internal processes are connected by the measures, and the sum of the functional measures is the measure of the process. Figure 5.1 shows that by measuring at each intersection, or handoff, the organization can ensure better results across the entire process.

To keep a process performing, it is important to determine what to focus on and measure these. Keep the focus on the customer values, and drive accountability back through all the functions. Keep this accountability visual, introduce pace and pitch, simplify, and drive improvement.

In lean development, the pace of development itself is established and measured by breaking the effort into smaller pieces. This is why breaking development into small learning cycles is so essential. It gives the team and the leadership a way to measure progress toward the overall goal. Leadership can determine if the project is on track when all of the learning cycles are on track. However, if a learning cycle is derailed in some way (a flow interrupter), leadership can take action and address the issue or remove the roadblock.

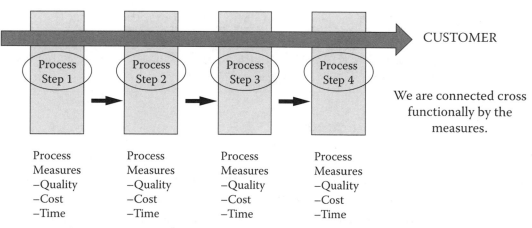

Figure 5.1 Functional silos in a value stream. Customer measures are the sum of the individual process measures.

Observing and checking on the progress of the learning cycles allow the leadership to take focused and direct corrective action on the problems that are bogging the team down. For this reason, each learning cycle is assessed to determine whether it is on time or overdue. When the learning cycle method is made visual by the team, the leadership can tell at a glance when the learning cycle is heading in the wrong direction. This is a key differentiator of the learning cycle method.

How to Evaluate Systemic Issues

There are some parts of a process that are hindered and held back by the same external factors every time. Some examples are the:

- Launch plan
- Engineering drawing revision control process
- Capital approval process
- Computer systems that do not align with each other, causing redundant efforts and data rekeying
- Funding for prototypes and models
- Prototyping process and resources needed to build them
- Resource availability and assignment to the project itself

If an organization experiences these systemic problems, they affect the process every time unless corrected. If there is a systemic issue that needs fixing, then no time should be wasted in attacking it. The longer the wait, the more frequently the waste will be encountered.

Plan-Do-Check-Act Sequence

Take any one of them and start work on it. For instance, if a variable resource model does not exist in the organization, allowing planning across all the teams so that resources can be easily flexed or moved, the solution is to apply lean thinking to the problem. Identify the problem and complete a Plan-Do-Check-Act sequence to solve the problem.

Plan

The resources in development should be planned by learning cycles, with the core team assigned to the project as 100% dedicated resources. As a learning cycle requires additional resources, the resources are assigned from a bullpen or moved from other teams. Techniques for rapidly moving resources are referred to as *swarming* or *agile* approaches. This variable resource model for design and development is a great problem solver, but it must be fully supported by management to succeed.

Do

A company usually has internal resources with the expertise to solve specific problems. If a learning cycle has identified the need for a resource that is not currently on the team, move the resource to the team for the duration of the learning cycle. Since learning cycles are typically only 3 to 4 weeks long, moving resources is not a huge drain on the part of the organization that is releasing a person to assist the team.

Teams should be encouraged to identify when they need resources outside the company. Perhaps no one in the company has the specific knowledge needed to solve the problem. An outside consultant can formally join a team, or (more preferably) the outside paid experts can be brought in for a specific learning cycle to answer questions related to the field of expertise. This can save money in consulting fees, because the consultants are only brought in for answering specific questions for a specified period.

Check

The end of the learning cycle is a perfect time to confirm that the additional resource brought into the learning cycle allowed the team to answer the unknown questions. If the team benefited from the consultant's knowledge and expertise, it will be reflected in the quality of the answers.

Act

Adjust the resource plans and reapply them to the next batch of learning cycles. If the resource reassignments for the learning cycles benefited the team, then repeat them for the next learning cycle. However, it is possible the resource plans and availability need adjustment. Perhaps the managers are reluctant to release the resources. If this is happening, the issue should be addressed for the next set of learning cycles. The goal should be to have a portion of the staff as flexible and ready to redeploy its expertise to whatever team needs help.

This kind of work on systemic issues often shows immediate results. With systemic problems, everyone feels the effect. That makes the results very visible, and the impact of solving the problems is larger. Think about attacking systemic issues as a great step toward success, especially early in the journey of innovative lean development. Often available as quick kills, these will build enthusiasm while benefiting the entire organization.

How to Control the Process

The question asked most often by people who are about to use learning cycles is, "How do you ensure that the leadership is aligned across the teams?" Learning cycles are fast paced, and full of action targeted toward completing development. However, with any effort that crosses over multiple teams, there will inevitably be conflict. Teams will have conflicting objectives, and decisions will be required to keep the process moving forward. What should an organization and its leadership do to drive the learning cycles? Whom will they use? Is one discipline suited to drive a learning cycle better than another?

The Role of a Development Council

As mentioned, some companies name a chief engineer who makes the key decisions and is responsible for the whole project. However, there is a more democratic system compatible with American business. Replace the chief engineer with a board of decision makers, a development council so to speak. The council will have representation by all the key disciplines, and they can make decisions jointly. A leader of the council is needed, but the sole responsibility for the decisions does not lie only with the leader.

The council will provide navigation aids to the team that is working through a learning cycle, removing the inevitable roadblocks and flow interrupters that need to be addressed rapidly by a decision-making group. In addition, if the project is made up of multiple subteams that all are working on the various subsystems, or elements, of the project, there will be points in the process when conflicts will need to be resolved. This, too, requires a decision-making group and the proper attention to roles across the team. When there are multiple subteams that must interconnect, the council can assist the teams to drive to a common solution. The decision-making body is typically a cross-functional team made up of the upper-level leaders who have responsibility for the project. They provide the tie-breaking votes when the team is unable to resolve questions, or when directional issues rise to the top.

The council can insist the teams use two key tools to ensure that development will happen on time and on budget. First, the teams must come together with a common build at the integration event. This means that before they go off and design their individual elements, the interface points among the teams must be very accurately defined, and the date of the integration build should be determined. Then, at the integration event, the teams are expected to show how their subelements will come together in an integrated fashion. This integration event helps to ensure that the teams are working toward the same goals.

Second, the teams need a tool to help them stay connected while they are off on their own learning cycles. To accomplish this, the council can appoint individuals who float across the teams and become commonly shared resources. Senior staff, who are recognized experts in their function, are excellent choices for this role. For example, the teams might have a senior designer, engineer, manufacturing specialist, and marketing expert who spend time with each team. They should be part of all the team updates, and should take key knowledge from one team and share it with the other teams. These floaters will resolve many interdependencies between the teams, and most issues will never need to reach the development council. Occasionally, the team of experts will need to raise decisions to a higher level. That is where the council is used.

The senior-level experts who have spent time with the multiple teams also represent the interests of the team to the development council. Since a learning cycle is on a very fast pace, the decision-making group must be available on very short notice. This can be done by setting aside time each week for the teams to bring their issues to the council. Once or twice a week should be enough. The important thing is for the decision makers to be available when the issues are brought forward. The experts will bring the issues to the council, explain their nature, and help the council understand the various trade-offs to be made. Once decisions are made at the council level, the experts representing the teams will bring the decisions back to the teams.

The development council members can also visit the team area looking for issues and flow interrupters that might require the upper-level decision makers to resolve. Remember, a lean-thinking leader is one who looks for problems where none is thought to exist. Therefore, while the council members are reviewing how well the process is working, they can also look for issues and problems that might be facing the team.

Think of governance of the project as an umbrella. The umbrella is protecting the team from all of the snow, rain, and sleet that might come down in the form of issues, flow interrupters, and organizational demands that do not bring any value to the project. That umbrella does not need to be up all of the time, but during the course of the project, it should be opened, covering the team to ensure that development can proceed uninterrupted. The role of the development council is to provide that umbrella to the team, and to hold it over them while it goes through the learning cycles.

The development council or the development leadership can also be alert to and help fix broken support processes. When a company first begins lean development, some of the supporting development processes will require immediate improvements. The overall time spent in development needs to be shortened, and the quality of the output needs to be improved. In order to understand what is actually happening in a development process, whether the development is in information technology or in product development, the leadership needs to understand how the process is malfunctioning.

The Role of Value Stream Mapping in Innovative Lean Development

It is a mistake to value stream map already documented development processes. The documentation for both IT and product development processes are typically very complete. However, mapping the existing process as documented gives neither a new view of how the process functions, nor a way to improve it in order to make it more functional, finish on time, or finish within budget.

Value stream maps that are drawn from the already documented process are really just another view of the same process. Neither the team nor its senior executives can learn anything new from this exercise. The maps just tell all involved what they already know; development takes a long time and often lacks discipline to follow the process.

The right place to start is with actual projects that have already gone through the process. When recently completed projects still fresh in everyone's minds are examined, the results of the value stream mapping exercise are completely different. The real story and all of the wastes in the development process are exposed.

Value stream map the project, not the process.

Innovative lean development embraces the lean principle of value stream mapping to expose and eliminate wastes. The lean principle's focus includes:

- Identifying value from the customer's perspective
- Identifying value streams that create value
- Making value streams flow, by identifying and eliminating waste
- Enabling the customer to pull value
- Striving for perfection by repeating this process until zero waste remains

Lean is an improvement system, and requires the lean practitioner to accurately know the current state of the value stream before attempting to improve the process. In lean development, value stream maps are drawn to understand the actual process and then leverage to create a future state value stream map that allows the team to initiate changes and improvement exercises.

Therefore, map to:

- Make the process visible
- Point to problems
- Focus direction

In almost every case, the value stream map is the first time people have seen the entire process end-to-end. Successful maps are drawn with specificity and detail.

Most organizations have a well-documented development system—a product development system, an information technology development and rollout system, and so on. These are typically very detailed project management lists, which have been built over many years of development, and following them will produce a product or program with every corporate *t* crossed and *i* dotted. These are also valuable procedures for completing and adhering to regulations and certifications. If a development group maps its process, it tends to get little more than a visual version of this project management list.

The power of mapping is to make the development visual, point to problems, and focus direction.

A much more effective way to take advantage of mapping is to value stream map a project, not the process. When real work is discussed and actual events are included, the picture is much more complete and accurate, yielding much more powerful results.

Working with a product development group whose management identifies development cycle durations as unacceptably long, the team knows what problems it is trying to solve. A good approach is to encourage the team to go further to show the true performance of the organization by mapping two different, recently completed projects; one of higher complexity and one of low to medium complexity. Generally, the higher complexity project will exhibit more problems, as might be expected, but together, the two maps will show striking similarities.

For example, when the product development phase gate (approval) process is overlaid on the map, it clarifies what the goal of each phase needs to be. As the workshop progresses, team members develop a template for future projects that focuses on a list of requirements to complete each phase; a kind of checklist for concept phase, for development phase, for pilot phase, and for production phase. The map points to problems in the current process—rework, waiting, and defects—and focuses the direction of leadership to manage what the project team should be working on at any point in the project. Leadership can now ask, "Is it on the checklist for this phase?" If it is, great; if not, work on something that is.

The checklists for the various phases of the development value stream map in Figure 5.2 help frame the team's work. Every company has its own milestones and knows what needs to be accomplished and when. Innovative lean development can be adapted to your organization and its development process.

Examples of items found on a product development checklist are:

- Financial projections
- Unit cost targets
- Supplier relationships
- Test plans
- Intellectual property reviews
- Quality assurance standards
- Business risk analysis

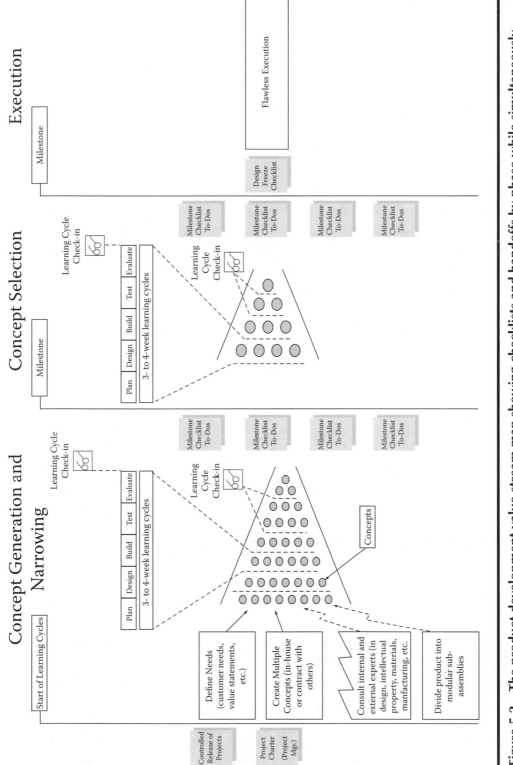

Figure 5.2   The product development value stream map showing checklists and handoffs by phase while simultaneously incorporating learning cycles.

An IT development checklist might include:

- Data architecture status
- Infrastructure (network and servers) status
- Security review
- System capacity analysis
- Web architecture status
- Business risk analysis
- Quality assurance standards

One of the outcomes of learning cycles should be the inclusion of objectives that answer whatever milestone deliverables your organization has identified. The learning cycle objectives, questions, and related tasks will help to uncover the answers that fulfill the milestone deliverables. Effective learning cycles include both milestone objectives and other learning objectives.

In our experience, the product development cycle duration for one group had been 18 to 24 months, and, after applying learning cycles, that group is completing projects in 8 to 12 months. Powerfully, value stream mapping an individual project allowed the team to dive deeper into the current process, point to the problems, and focus the direction in a way the process value stream map could not.

Therefore, make the process visible by mapping the projects that go through the process, and map it so that it will show what needs to be exposed. Map from a specific standpoint, use what is familiar and real, and focus on the common handoffs in the process. Mapping a project is the practical solution to successful value stream mapping in development.

Case Study: How to Map Development

The following example is fictional, but much of it may sound familiar to those in product development. All references to actual events are coincidental.

As you read this case study, determine what the steps in the process are. For clarity, the steps have been italicized.

Stu's Product Development

Stu Stucky owns a small office chair business. He has decided that his business is missing a lower-price point segment of the market typically found in the bigger office chain stores. He doesn't want to sacrifice good design, and he realizes that his current product development process takes too long; currently, his product development team uses a traditional phase gate process and manages their efforts with large Microsoft Project schedules. Historically, it has taken them 12 to 18 months to develop a new chair. The window of opportunity for Stu to develop a new chair is 6 to 9 months. Stu has decided to value stream map his development process to understand where it might be improved because he knows the team needs to reach the development tollgate within 4 months.

The sequence begins when marketing gathers customer requirements. Jim, from the marketing department, *gathers competitive research*. He *compiles a business case*, summarizing requirements, volume projections, and the price point for the new chair. Sally from industrial design (who has been doing her own research) receives the business case and *develops initial concept models*. After a 2-week delay due to scheduling conflicts, Jim *validates the new chair concept* with the dealers. Stu and the team hold their *phase 1 tollgate review* and decide to move ahead. Doug, a senior seating engineer, then takes the business case and validation report and *engineers the chair*, requesting several changes from design and marketing during the design process.

Nancy, Stu's most experienced operations engineer, receives the engineering design from Doug and stacks it in her 3-week backlog of projects. Next, she and her team *plan and execute a development run* in the plant. Nancy recommends multiple changes to Doug. Doug takes the chairs to the test lab, which has a 1-week backlog, where the *chairs are tested* by David for 3 weeks. The tests uncover one failure and one safety concern.

Jim rushes to *make changes to the design and cost model* in 1 week so the team can *hold the development tollgate review.*

This is Stu's development process, and he is desperate to improve it. However, to improve processes, we must be able to measure them. There are four standard time measures and a quality measure.

- *Process Time (P/T):* The time spent doing value-added work (heads-down time, time spent on the work on the desktop, or touch time). Example: Gathering the data needed for the generation of a report takes 30 minutes.
  P/T = 30 minutes
- *Cycle Time through a Process (C/T):* The elapsed time for a unit of work to move through a process box, including the process time. It is

measured from the time the unit of work enters the process to the time
it leaves the process complete, including all value-added and non-value-
added time. The unit of work might be an order, a quote, a drawing, a
claim, and so on.
Example: 30 minutes to gather the information needed is spread
over 1 full day due to multitasking on other activities and multiple
interruptions.
C/T = 1 day

■ *Queue Time or Wait Time (W/T):* The time that work sits in a queue or
inbox before it enters the process.
Example: The request to gather the data for this report sits in an
e-mail inbox for 2 days before anyone works on it.
W/T = 2 days

■ *Total Cycle Time:* Cycle time + wait time = Total C/T. The time to complete the entire value stream, including all cycle times and wait times.
In this example: 1-day cycle time plus 2-day wait time
1-day C/T + 2-day W/T = 3-day total C/T

Notice that this is 3 days of total cycle time for 30 minutes of actual process time. This may be difficult to accept, but it is quite common in office
processes.

■ *Percent Complete and Accurate (%C&A):* Is defined as the measure of
the first pass yield or as an estimate of the quality of the work as it is
received. What percentage of the time can the work be acted upon and
passed along without questions, clarifications, or rework?
If one out of four needs clarification, the rework is 25%.
%C&A = 75%
With these five measures, a baseline of the current state can be established to evaluate any process.

Now back to Stu Stucky and his broken process. For the one and only time,
the data set will be given for measuring a process. Typically, in real-life
implementations of lean process improvements, this kind of information is
gathered by observation and interviews. It is what is called homework, and
it is a critical part of successful process improvement.

For Stu's seating product development, consider the following process
data set. This is the information needed to create the map:

- Gather Competitive Research: Jim (Marketing)
  - P/T = 20 hours
  - C/T = 3 weeks
  - W/T = 0
  - %C&A = 50%
- Compile Business Case: Jim
  - P/T = 6 hours
  - C/T = 4 days (multitasking on other tasks)
  - W/T = 0
  - %C&A = 70%
- Develop Initial Concepts: Sally (Industrial Design)
  - P/T = 80 hours
  - C/T= 3 weeks
  - W/T = 1 week
  - %C&A = 50%
- Validate New Chair Concept: Jim
  - P/T = 20 hours
  - C/T = 2 weeks
  - W/T = 2 weeks
  - %C&A = 80%
- Phase Gate 1 Review: Team and Stu
  - P/T = 2 hours
  - C/T = 2 hours
  - W/T = 5 days (scheduling conflicts)
  - %C&A = 90%
- Engineer the Chair: Doug (Engineering)
  - P/T = 60 hours
  - C/T = 4 weeks (multitasking)
  - W/T = 0
  - %C&A = 80%
- Development Run: Nancy (Operations)
  - P/T = 200 hours
  - C/T= 7 weeks
  - W/T = 3 weeks
  - %C&A = 90%
- Test Chair: David (Test Lab)
  - P/T = 100 hours
  - C/T = 3 weeks

   - W/T = 1 week (backlog of testing)
   - %C&A = 90%
- Make Changes and Complete Cost Model: Doug
   - P/T = 45 hours
   - C/T = 2 weeks
   - W/T = 0
   - %C&A = 80%
- Phase Gate 2 Review: Team and Stu
   - P/T = 2 hours
   - C/T = 2 hours
   - W/T = 1 day
   - %C&A = 90%

The standard lean icons are used to represent outside suppliers, process boxes, and data boxes. In addition, the idea of iterations, inboxes, and wait time also have accepted icons. The goal here is to communicate the value stream map to anyone who may view it. Accepted lean icons help standardize this (see Figure 5.3).

All of this information is used to create a value stream map, using lean icons to represent the suppliers, process boxes, and data boxes. The following eight steps provide guidance to create a map.

1. Identify the manufacturing plant using the icon for the external source in the upper right hand corner.
2. Identify the customer/dealer and draw the icon in the upper left hand corner on the map. Use the same icon.
3. From the data set, identify the process steps, draw the process boxes below the customer icons, going left to right horizontally across the map. Inside the box, label the process steps (include a verb and noun phrase, for example, the phrase "send memo," to indicate the action performed in the work). There are 10 process steps in Stu's process map (see Figure 5.4).
4. Use the icon for the data box and draw one under each process box. Fill with selected data attributes.
5. Using the appropriate icons, indicate where work may be accumulating or waiting.
6. Indicate how the work moves among the process steps. Is it push, pull, flow?
7. Indicate where and how information is moved through the process.

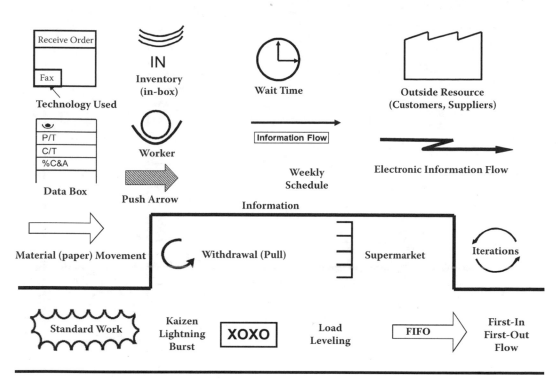

Figure 5.3   Standard lean mapping icons.

8. Draw the timeline across the bottom of the map to show total project time.
   - P/T = Process Time: The time spent doing value-added work. (The time spent on the work on the desktop.)
   - W/T = Wait Time: In a case where the product is waiting a day for the process step to occur, show it as a Wait Time of "1 day."
   - C/T = Cycle Time: In a case where the process activity is spread out over a period of 3 hours during a process step, show as a Cycle Time of "3 hours."
   - ■ Tally your Process Time (value-added time)
   - ■ Tally your Cycle Time (non-value-added time)
   - ■ Tally your Wait Time (non-value-added time)
   - ■ Tally your Total Cycle Time (= C/T + W/T)
   - ■ Tally your total %C&A by multiplying the individual entries of %C&A.

Using all of this, spend some time following and identifying these eight steps in the following value stream map for Stu's Seating. The idea is to

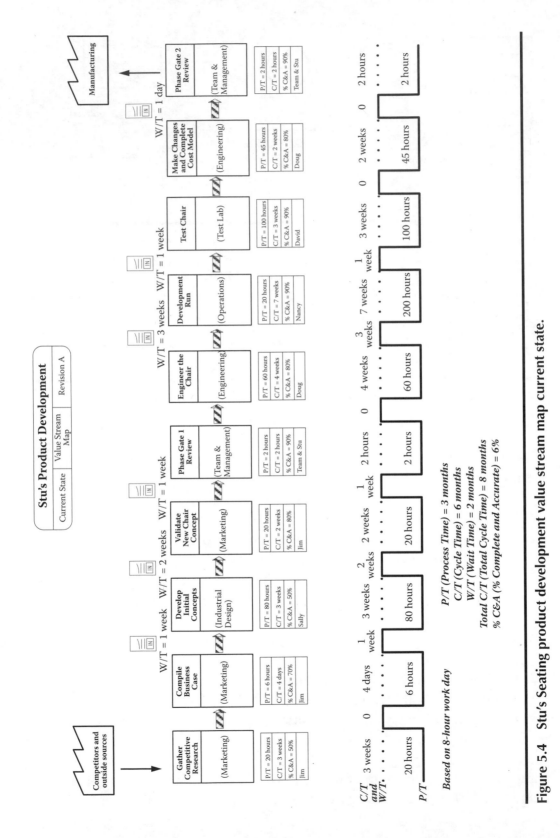

Figure 5.4 Stu's Seating product development value stream map current state.

practice value stream mapping skills frequently to really learn and apply the techniques.

The Impact of Supporting Processes

Other discoveries can occur when mapping projects; additional low-hanging fruit can be identified and addressed. When systemic issues were introduced earlier in this chapter, the issues that touch the value stream every time were highlighted as potential targets for improvement. Of course, issues that happen less often can still present big problems. These result from troubles and problems in the supporting processes. Examples of supporting processes are:

- Processes to build tooling either offshore or closer to the point of manufacture
- Prototyping shop or model-making resources
- Test lab or testing resources
- Prototyping methods
- Outsourced design resources

When projects need an accelerated timeline to deliver multiple designs in product development, what options exist to accomplish this? For example, what if the internal design group does not have resource availability, but could help manage the overall direction? Another approach might be to partner with a number of outside design groups, giving them all the requirements, and asking them to submit solutions, working in parallel to deliver workable solutions. A kind of bake-off with established partners would result in multiple solutions from which to pick, play off against one another, and further develop. This method utilizes set-based design by developing multiple concepts, while simultaneously minimizing the waste of waiting. This approach gives a tremendous boost to the learning cycles by fixing a supporting process to the overall value stream.

   When value stream mapping a development process, be sure to include the supporting processes, since they touch the project all along the way. Some of these are outside the organization, but many of them are internal. As a lean-thinking organization, identify these as potential areas for improvement and put together improvement plans. Taking the opportunity to improve these areas will pay dividends every time there is a need to repeat the process. Focus on improvement, but look to be collaborative. Problem solve in teams for best results. The process is the customer here; what does your process value in these circumstances? Be certain to define value and minimize waste in the value stream.

Innovative lean development requires focus on the process. Lean processes are tightly linked, and like an ecosystem, any element change affects the whole—by design. Value stream maps make the process failures and waste visible, and embracing these is the key to continuous improvement. Process focus is essential for lean results, because stable processes produce improved results. Be sure to take care of the process, and the process will take care of you.

The Ideal Future State: Working toward a "Perfect" System

After creating a current state value stream map and identifying the supporting processes needing improvement, the value stream mapper will be ready to build the ideal future state, which can also be described as a map with the end in view for the development organization. The future state is just that—always in the future. The current state is just another step toward the ideal of a perfectly functioning system.

Each step toward an ideal future state takes work and time to accomplish. Through the implementation of multiple process improvements, what the Japanese call *kaizens* (kaizen is loosely translated as "good change"), measurable improvements are realized. Typically, a number of kaizens are identified, and subteams are formed to investigate and implement them. Along the way, more and more wastes are uncovered, and more improvements are realized.

The goal is to improve continuously, identifying new areas for incremental advancement on the way to the ideal. Look again at the future state development map (Figure 5.2) with a more educated eye. Figure 5.5 illustrates the first phase of the future state map shown in Figure 5.2.

Notice there is a checklist for accomplishing the desired goals at the end of each phase (including this one); two kaizens are identified to help achieve the ideal state. (More kaizens are identified all the time, and they become the drivers of continuous improvement.) Along the way, companies need to tackle their internal, structural issues that affect their performance; at the same time, they must address some supporting processes. These might include the cost and timing for offshore versus domestic tooling or

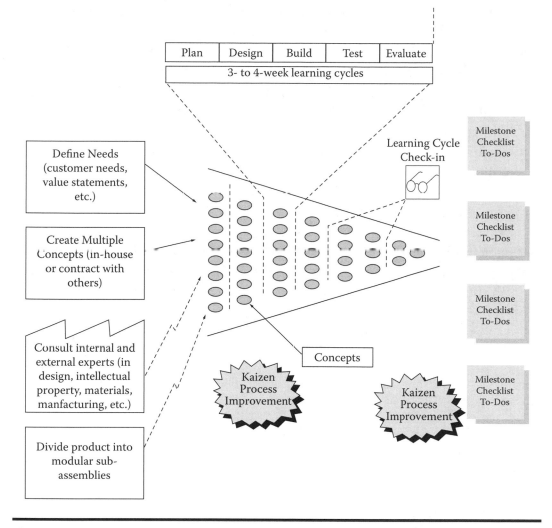

Figure 5.5   Future state development map.

the overall engineering or software release process. Completing kaizens to make the process more lean and innovative is a journey, and over time, the cultural shift in the organization will become evident. The journey embraces discovery and process improvement to move the organization toward becoming a lean organization.

To achieve the ideal future state, an organization must:

▪ *Measure the Process:* Results are important, but the lean leader wants to produce them in the leanest way possible. Decide what measures are important to keep this process producing, and focus on them; and don't measure things that are not important.

■ *Fix Systemic Issues:* Issues that affect many or all value streams are defined as systemic issues. Innovative lean development is looking to minimize all issues that affect performance, but systemic ones have a bright light shining on them every time the process passes by. Identify and attack these for the best overall impact.

■ *Value Stream Map Projects, Not the Process:* Using value stream maps will make the process visible, point to problems, and focus direction. It starts with visibility. The best way to make a process visible is to value stream map a project that has recently passed through the process. Since it is what the process produces, mapping a project is familiar, specific, and most useful.

■ *Fix the Supporting Processes:* Most processes have supporting processes. As the work flows along the value stream, there are many inputs along the way. These inputs are the result of other value streams that support the process. In mapping, do not forget to show the supporting processes, and be sure to focus on them to achieve better results.

Chapter 6

How to Implement a Knowledge Capture and Retrieval System

"Organizations with high levels of technical knowledge, a clear transformation plan involving a change in management behavior, and a high level of energy have yokoten, the term Toyota uses for the horizontal transfer of information and knowledge across an organization."

James Womack, founder and chairman,
Lean Enterprise Institute

The idea for a product knowledge capture and sharing came out of lean development efforts, which recognized the need to store key knowledge as it was uncovered by various teams during the learning cycles. Learning organizations all use knowledge capture and sharing as a way to promote learning and problem solving. Toyota developed a very complete library of design knowledge and checklists for automobiles that has become known as the "know-how" database.*

There are other excellent examples of knowledge management systems in the public domain. The government space agency, NASA, has an

---

* James P. Womack, Daniel T. Jones, and Daniel Roos. *The Machine That Changed the World: The Story of Lean Production.*

outstanding site open to the public, which captures knowledge gained from its many space initiatives. The quest for many companies is to move from a situation where no or little knowledge is capture and shared, to an environment where sharing knowledge becomes part of the corporate DNA.

If learning cycles are thought of as the scientific method with a hypothesis statement and experiments to prove or disprove the hypothesis, capturing the knowledge from a learning cycle is equivalent to documenting the results and conclusions of scientific experiments. For this reason, capturing, storing, and using the knowledge gained should be part of the culture in a lean organization.

Knowledge captured in development is important because "the most important wastes [to avoid] in development are wastes of knowledge," and the generation of knowledge is a key deliverable of the development process.* In the innovative lean development method, there is a natural fit between the cycles of discovery and capturing the knowledge that comes from the prototyping and learning that occur within the learning cycles. The innovative lean development method sets up the learning experiment by stating that the way to maximize the customer's wants and minimize the wastes is to close the gaps between where a team is and where it needs to be. The gaps defined are similar to the hypothesis in the scientific experiment.

To address these gaps, the team utilizes repeated learning cycles for continuous feedback of discovery and to increase the velocity (or pace) of that discovery in development. Implementing learning cycles is essential to achieve results; what happened inside the learning cycles may soon be forgotten and abandoned. What is needed to enhance the organization's memory is a formal process of recording the results of the learning cycle.

For knowledge to be captured and retrieved, the whole organization needs to be aware and informed of the ways that the organization expects every individual to communicate what is learned. Companies and their leadership need to define their own best practices of knowledge capture and retrieval, but the basic formula should remain framed as, "Will the knowledge generated be useful to the rest of the company, and how can it be shared so the rest of the organization can use this new discovery?"

---

* Al Ward. *Lean Product and Process Development*, p. 30.

How to Create a Knowledge Culture

Although innovation leverages new ideas from existing knowledge whenever it can, it is common that knowledge capture remains low on any team's priority list. Capturing knowledge requires a fair amount of discipline. The team must learn the new practices and habits for documenting and sharing what has been learned during the learning cycles. Ideas should be captured as well. Then future developers will benefit from the discoveries made by previous teams. Innovative lean development will truly show success only when the development culture goes through a revolution in the way members identify the problems and solve them; in the way they capture and communicate the discoveries; in the very approach to how they think and the habits formed in sharing knowledge. Innovative lean development needs to become a way of life that turns an organization into problem solvers who capture and share what they have learned.

In Chapter 8, the concept of changing behaviors, practices, and habits, which are the engine that drives change in the underlying culture, is developed. Three key ways to help the team convert to a knowledge-based culture are to:

1. Capture learning as it is created.
2. Capture ideas as they occur.
3. Share knowledge beyond the immediate team.

Each part of this trio is required to ensure learning is attained in the organization.

How to Capture Learning as It Is Created

Each team member participates in the creation of knowledge, but, too often, the knowledge is shared verbally and rarely recorded. Such knowledge is quickly lost. People often do not recall what they discovered or learned on the last project, or even during the last learning cycle.

Project team members look at the capturing of knowledge as added work during the development cycle because of the time required to document and publish the ideas. However, innovative problem solvers approach work differently. True problem solvers know that a gap between the goal and the status quo needs to be identified and held open for the team to explore. They understand that it clarifies the work that needs to be done and that a clearly stated gap, or problem statement, brings clarity to the team and helps them apply problem-solving techniques. Finally, the accurate problem-solving technique that is part of a learning cycle sets up the opportunity to identify, capture, and share the knowledge that was gained during the activities of that cycle.

To turn an organization into learners, management should ask members questions. For example, managers can help by asking the team at the close of each learning cycle, "What did you learn?" Furthermore, leaders should require the team to capture the learning in a central location. If none exists, management should create a central storage area for knowledge. It does not have to be complicated or sophisticated, just functional.

The best opportunity to capture knowledge is at the close of the learning cycles. The learning cycle scope document includes a section reserved for the capture of new knowledge. Another important technique is to capture the answers to each question that is included in the scope document at the beginning of the learning cycle. At the end of the cycle, the team should record all knowledge gained during the learning cycle.

The shift of looking for answers instead of results is a key concept in lean development. All teams seeking to solve or discover solutions to problems in the early concept phases should seek "truth finding."* Finding the truth about the requirements and feasibility of the solution sets is an important step toward creating an elegant and simple solution to meet the values of the customer.

How to Capture Ideas as They Occur

Besides capturing the knowledge at the end of the learning cycles, ideas that are generated throughout the learning cycle should also be captured. Raw ideas can be captured in an idea storehouse, allowing the team to go back later to pick ideas that have been considered and perhaps tried. As discussed earlier, common techniques for capturing ideas include recording results from brainstorming sessions or with some other idea capture tool. Regardless of the method, the importance is to log the ideas in a way

---

* Eric Bonabeau, et al. A More Rational Approach to New-Product Development. *Harvard Business Review*, p. 96, March 2008.

that will make them easy to find in the future. Waiting is a lean waste, as is searching for hard to find information. Therefore, when ideas are captured, they should be indexed and retrievable.

Standardize and Share Knowledge

The goal of yokoten is the horizontal transfer of information and knowledge across an organization. Lean leaders will encourage the team to share what they have learned. Leaders should set an expectation for the practice of sharing ideas and knowledge gained. It is only when information is shared that the organization will actually benefit from the learning activities of the team.

Teams should not have to create the method for capturing the knowledge; instead, the standard formats for capturing knowledge should be defined and standardized across the organization. Several tools are available to help collect, combine, and catalog ideas. They allow innovation to be structured, provide a repository for the methodical use of generated ideas, and help the user do a job more efficiently, not create more work. Basic, easy to use, and readily available are good descriptors for the best tool.

A structured way to capture ideas, along with an easy way to find the solutions later, is needed. There are multiple ways to capture ideas—one team used a wall of sticky notes to keep the ideas before it, another logged its ideas on a computer. A matrix is a great place to collect ideas. Whatever method is employed, the key here is to record the ideas and have them available for future reference.

Concept Selection Matrix Method

Use a matrix, at least to start, that will help catalog and organize collected thoughts, ideas, and solutions. Readily available spreadsheets are a great first step to record all of the ideas discovered throughout each learning cycle. A matrix also provides an effective way to evaluate a number of ideas. In one matrix, for example, the customer's attributes, focusing on the customer wants, might be listed across the top of a spreadsheet. The team's ideas are then listed down the left side, and ratings can be placed inside each cell. Ratings capture how well the ideas maximize the customer's wants giving a clearer view to which ideas have the most merit. Similarly, rating how the ideas minimize waste gives a road map for value-added activities. The benefits are:

■ The matrix allows many ideas to be evaluated at once, giving a clear picture of better solutions.
■ The rating in the matrix provides a historical record for future reference of which concepts (or ideas) best fit the needs.

In Figure 6.1, leading concepts are listed on the left side of the matrix, and the customer wants, organizational wants, and other wants (physical restrictions, manufacturing standards, IT system requirements, etc.) appear across the top. Each concept is rated against the wants listed at the top. The categories of wants can be customized to fit the situation; however, the customer's wants are always listed first.

Organizational wants are listed for a product or service being considered. Other categories capture the things that the end product or service must include or rules it must follow. A principle of physics, such as gravity or "two objects cannot occupy the same space at the same time" cannot be denied, and the product designed must meet these criteria. Therefore, the needs placed under a category of physics are the things that the final innovation must follow.

Initially, the team may list only a few concepts, but during the evaluation of each concept on the selection matrix, the deficiencies of the ideas will become immediately apparent. Very soon, the team will use its new knowledge of what fulfills the needs and what does not to generate additional ideas.

	Customer Wants			Organizational Wants			Other Wants			Overall
	Need 1	Need 2	Need 3	Need 1	Need 2	Need 3	Need 1	Need 2	Need 3	
Concept A	Rating	Rating	etc.							
Concept B	Rating	Rating	etc.							
Concept C	Rating	Rating	etc.							

Figure 6.1 Matrix with ratings of leading concepts against key attributes.

The use of the concept selection matrix is effective during the initial learning cycles of a project (see Chapter 3). At this stage, the team is looking for new concepts and it needs a way to capture and compare the ideas. A matrix approach is a great tool to have in the lean development toolbox.*

Knowledge Capture A3 Method

Lean companies use an A3 size (metric paper size, close to 11 × 17 inches) one-page document for knowledge capture. This is a standard format, with a rich history from many lean companies including Toyota and Honda. A detailed example and instructions for how to use this form can be found in Appendix B.

Several pieces of information help to document the knowledge in an A3 format:

- Clear statement of the problem to be solved
- Historical background on the problem
- Root cause analysis of the reason for the problem
- References, sources, or experts consulted
- Brief description of any current work (or countermeasure)
- Detailed list of trade-offs or trade-off curves describing the different variables and options

The author of any A3 knowledge capture document seeks to describe the problem and the research done to solve it with enough detail that the reader can easily understand and trace the work that was done to solve it.

Think again of the scientific method. The scientist, in a hypothesis statement, seeks to describe the nature of the problem, and proceeds to describe the experiment and the results in enough detail so that any other scientist familiar with the field can re-create the results and validate the findings. Similarly, the lean innovator seeks to describe in detail the problem to be solved, how it was done, and the results achieved or discovered.

Finally, the scientist describes the results in the conclusion of the report. The conclusion captures the findings and claims of the hypothesis, shows how the findings apply to other investigators' hypotheses, and tries to extend the results to other experiments that could be completed by others in the

---

* Bart Huthwaite has greatly enhanced and perfected this approach with the InnovationCUBE™, which we recommend to you. Bart Huthwaite, *Lean Design Solutions*.

future. In the same way, the knowledge captured from the learning cycles must be stated so the results relate to other discoveries made and extend to future learning cycles. The knowledge is captured at the end of each learning cycle to document what was just learned, and to inform the next learning cycle where to turn next.

A common risk of development is that a high degree of uncertainty exists in hitting the end dates because it is difficult to predict an accurate timeline for discoveries. Using the concepts in innovative lean development, the teams embrace the process of making discoveries, and the team members will let each completed learning cycle inform the next learning cycles. The discoveries are captured as knowledge, documented by the team, and then used to plan the next learning cycle. When the focal point is on the problems at hand, the right resources are applied to the problem, and, when the knowledge gained in the last learning cycle is captured and referenced during future learning cycles, resources are not expended needlessly on tasks that are outside of the current focus area.

Store Knowledge for Easy Access

Some companies are now piloting the idea that a technology system similar to Wikipedia can be used to capture key product knowledge. The hypothesis is that an online location for information storage written by the people who created knowledge is the best way to gather and share knowledge and ideas. Today, knowledge management sites are being developed internally to allow knowledge workers to post their findings. The sites also allow peer-to-peer editing as necessary to ensure information accuracy, and, as is true with the popular Wikipedia system, which is in the public domain, these internal systems use editors, or knowledge experts, to ensure the quality and accuracy of the information stored. The idea is to promote knowledge capture and sharing across the organization.

A Wikipedia-style storage solution allows information to be stored and linked to other information. Links can be created by relating other articles and documents from elsewhere in the company, creating an internal web of information. The links can also point to other external locations to bring in expert data or standards. This expands the internal network to the external world as well, creating what can be a much broader network of information.

Individuals post entries using a web-hosting tool. Restrictions for authoring are limited to just a few key things, but some structure is needed to organize entries for later retrieval. Besides a simple form for organizing the entries, the online system also organizes entries using some basic categories. Information can be grouped by categories, materials, part names, products, or alert tags. The entry of information should be simple and easy so that everyone will use the tool.

The goal of the online knowledge repository is easy searching so that information can be retrieved by all of the groups involved with development. Keywords can help to narrow the search by popping that information to the top of the search list. However, the search is not restricted to the keywords or categories created. Normally, underlying the technology is an open search engine that will find any document that includes words in the search string.

The team working on developing a workable yet simple knowledge Wiki should include people from information technology, an expert in library science, potential users, plus members of an implementation team.

How to Build a Knowledge Capture System

The first step is to build a pilot system to experiment in capturing knowledge information for an organization. Information from a few sources can be requested from individuals already involved in lean pilots. A letter of introduction from a leader is a great way to start (see Figure 6.2).

Determining what information to store on a knowledge management site requires asking a series of questions about the authors and potential content. Here are some questions to start with:

Is there a standard way for entering knowledge? Standard work is one of the cornerstones of any lean system, and standard work for the capture of knowledge is no exception. The entry page for the knowledge captured should have a common look and feel. It is no accident that all of the Wikipedia entries have a similar look and feel. The internal site for a company should also have a standardized look. Many companies use the A3 templates, which are great starting points, but can be somewhat redundant with the electronic Wiki pages (which already have a format and structure).

What kind of work does each of the authors do? Are they all design engineers who would work interchangeably on teams, or do they have specialties? What are they all working on?

The goal is to let a group of editors know who the authors are and what they are working on. This is a distinct advantage of an internal system

---

Subject: Product Knowledge Wiki Entries

Team,

In our lean development journey and in the spirit of continuous improvement, please be ready to provide content for the knowledge capture site that is being developed.

You will be contacted by our site editor [name] to provide any product and design knowledge content that we have acquired, and [he/she] will help format the information.

This will be a great help to all of us as we learn and begin to use the Wiki site in new product development to "jump start" our understanding of the questions in learning cycles.

Thank you for your support,

[Name]

Director, Engineering and Development

Figure 6.2   Sample letter of invitation activities.

compared to the web version of Wikipedia, where the editors and authors do not know each other. On an internal company site, the authors and editors can and should know what the others are working on. An added benefit is that subject matter experts will soon emerge from the pool of authors posting knowledge to the site, who can be readily reached by e-mail or phone.

How frequent are the learning cycles, and how many exist between major milestones or phase gates? Anywhere from 2 to 10 learning cycles in a phase is typical. There will be more learning cycles in the early phases of the process, because these will typically be the shortest, just 2 to 3 weeks in length. Later learning cycles may be longer because the prototyping is more involved.

Is there a diagram or value stream map that depicts learning cycles? The process should be described by a learning cycle process diagram, or future state value stream map. The builder of the internal knowledge management site might consider creating an entry about lean development with reference diagrams, charts, and other standard forms and aids.

How do learning cycles open, proceed, and close? Every learning cycle should include a scope document that is built at the start of the learning cycle. It lists the learning objectives and then for each objective a series of questions (or discoveries) to be made in the learning cycle. These questions provoke thought about what knowledge should be captured.

How do learning cycles relate to phase gates? Is knowledge captured only at phase gates? There can be multiple learning cycles in each phase of the phase gate process, and knowledge should be captured at the end of each cycle. A phase gate is nothing more than the close of another learning cycle. The last learning cycle may include more project-related tasks, but there will also be significant learning happening because the team is trying to close out a phase of the project.

Can everyone on the site post to it? This is a basic question. While not everyone can post, everyone should have access to the information on the site. Teams benefit from reviewing their learning objectives for a project and posting learning for those objectives. Scheduled meetings to review objectives and lessons learned, such as integration events, are natural points in time to post learning.

Typically, the answers in the learning cycle scope document are rather cryptic; therefore, they should be expanded for the Wiki site, and should include the trade-offs, engineering analysis, historical research completed, and the conclusions reached at the end of the learning cycle.

Note that not every answered question is global knowledge; some answers are only pertinent to the team or the specific project.

Would it be appropriate to ask the learning cycle participants to review learning objectives for some number of recent past learning cycles, and post any documents related to those objectives? There is definitely opportunity to document learning from recently completed learning cycles. A discipline to immediately capture knowledge at the completion of any learning cycle should be fostered.

Is there a template for the learning cycle scope document? The learning cycle process needs a good template that lists the objectives of the learning cycle (or the gaps that need to be closed). It should also list in detail all of the questions that need to be answered indicating an assigned owner responsible for answering the question, although they will most likely ask for the help of others on the team.

How is the knowledge capture document used? Some of these documents are in PowerPoint files, others in Excel. What is the difference? Undoubtedly, there will be many different types of information, which may be stored at multiple locations, using various methods. The goal is to get to a single standard. That is why the initial definition of the site is so important. Both the entry form and the organization of the information should be standardized prior to rolling out the solution. A good site editor should be appointed for the review and oversight of the information posted to the knowledge management site.

How much knowledge might exist in past learning cycles that has not been posted? Past learning cycles represent a rich area to be mined for additional information. The knowledge gained may or may not be captured in the learning cycle scope documents; interviews with the engineers and designers might be required.

If knowledge capture documents aren't created routinely, is that because engineers lack the time or because most of the learning is too fragmentary or transient to capture or just not important enough? People are not always disciplined in their approaches, but the practice and behavior that should be fostered is to be disciplined in capturing the knowledge. Perhaps when the group is in the thick of making the discoveries and creating the knowledge, the members do not think about capturing it. It has not yet become routine. Management should encourage the leadership of the area to put an item in their weekly to-do lists to remind the teams to capture the knowledge. This is a form of standard work for the leadership. If they are requesting it of their teams, then the developers will post knowledge from the learning cycles in their current projects.

With answers to all of these questions, and with the creation of a good pilot system for capturing knowledge, the quest for knowledge to be captured and shared can begin. The set of questions is not meant to be exhaustive, but it does represent important items to consider. A final question that often comes up is whether initiatives like an electronic knowledge capture site should be grassroots led or leadership driven. In fact, both are required. The grassroots knowledge authors and editors have to find the site usable and beneficial, and the leadership has to ask their staff to capture knowledge. The capture of knowledge should be part of the employee's performance expectations from the start. With grassroots support, coupled with leadership expectations that knowledge captured is a must-do for the organization, the capture of knowledge will begin and grow exponentially.

There are four keys to capturing knowledge:

1. *Capture knowledge as it is created:* In a learning organization, knowledge represents resources. Lost knowledge means wasted resources; therefore, an organization must utilize every resource fully. As stewards of information assets, be disciplined and systematic about capturing new knowledge for future use.

2. *Capture ideas as they occur:* Ideas are the seeds of knowledge, and can mature into great ideas for innovation. The idea generator can be the seedbed for future solutions. Like knowledge, ideas are a company's future currency; collect, use, build, and protect them wisely.

3. *Share knowledge beyond the team:* Better ideas come from more collaboration, so spread knowledge across the enterprise. As an organization grows into a learning organization, experience predicts that ideas feed other ideas, and knowledge captured and shared will feed new knowledge. Sharing what has been learned increases the rate of discovery and maximizes the innovative jumps that the development organization will make.

4. *Store knowledge for easy access:* Information persistence describes situations where information, including books, project folders, and so on, is always available, visible, and accessible for easy reference or use. Similarly, problem-solving organizations must make newly discovered knowledge visible, accessible, and easy to use.

Chapter 7

The Role of Rapid Prototyping in Development

"There is no such thing as a failed experiment, only experiments with unexpected outcomes."

Buckminster Fuller, engineer and architect

Better speed to market requires better development speed, which results from quick, iterative learning cycles to embed innovation and agility into the development process.

If learning cycles are the heart of innovative lean development, then prototyping is the soul of innovative lean development. If increasing development speed is the goal, rapid prototyping is the vehicle. In every way, teams need to "get physical fast" because a prototype communicates visually in a way words or concept descriptions cannot, and therefore teach a team an enormous amount about the concept and design. In addition, customer validation, a critical portion of lean development feedback, is virtually impossible without prototypes.

Prototyping means different things to different organizations; it also takes on different meanings in different departments within the same organization. It is not unusual, for example, for engineering prototypes to be very hard to distinguish from production parts. It is usually the case that engineers, who are very close to the product, want to have the solution completely worked out before prototyping it. This is admirable, but it is not necessary, and it definitely does not contribute to development speed. In fact, it does the opposite. If the solutions are all worked out before they are shown to anyone, there is no time for feedback and adjustment. The primary way to reduce risks in development is to prototype the ideas quickly, allowing the team to test those ideas against project goals and customer wants.

How to Reduce Risks Inherent in Product Development

Product development is inherently a risky business. Not only will the solution be something new to the marketplace, often the team is pushing the envelope of an immature design, as well as an immature process where much is unknown. Questions about the product at the formative stage include:

- How will it perform?
- How will it be maintained?
- How durable should it be?
- Will it be affordable?
- Will it portray an image that attracts buyers?

These questions should look familiar. They come from the value statements the team defined at the beginning of the project.

Process questions also need to be answered:

- How will it be built?
- Where will it be built?
- What are the labor costs involved in building it?

All of these questions should be asked to make sure that the drivers of wastes are eliminated from the design.

Other risks include correctly solving the wrong problem and solving the right problem in the wrong way. One of the most effective ways to manage these risks is to get frequent, regular validation from customers and stakeholders. An organization cannot afford to get all the way through an expensive development effort, only to have the so-called solution rejected in the marketplace.

Step 1: Quickly Prototype to Solve Development Problems

Development is the messy part of a product launch because of all the things that are not known at the beginning. Rapid prototyping can answer questions about function, mass, wobble, weight, aesthetics, user needs, and so on. Prototypes do not have to be pretty; but they do have to answer our questions.

Step 2: Use Multiple Prototyping Techniques

Every project has an immovable deadline, and the design team is going to need every advantage to accomplish it. Prototypes are leveraged to reflect the level of the solution. Early in the project, the team is carrying multiple unproven concepts forward. For this reason, there is very little or no confidence in the solutions. At this early stage, just showing sketches of products or screen shots of IT solutions to stakeholders is sufficient. As the project progresses, the team receives more validation and gains more confidence; therefore, as requirements dictate, the prototypes should become more sophisticated. This leads to increasingly better decision making.

Step 3: Test the Prototypes

It is crucial that all prototypes be tested in order to get proper feedback. Again, the tests will take different forms as the project progresses. Early in the project, the tests may be as simple as showing sketches to customers. Informal physical or subsystem testing takes place as the concepts are refined, and full testing and evaluation is reserved for later, when only a few concepts remain.

Rapid, iterative prototyping enables a team to speed up development by showing the project stakeholders how something might look, rather than exactly how it will look. By obtaining feedback early and often, the maximum time is allowed for adjustment and the whole development process is much less expensive.

How to Use Quick Prototyping to Solve Development Problems

Innovative lean development embraces the idea of rapid learning cycles to optimize learning. The function of these short development bursts is to iterate quickly so development teams can increase speed. Effective development requires prototyping to determine direction and refine definition. Rapid development, then, requires rapid prototyping.

As seen previously, learning cycles break the work into smaller chunks, so discovery can take place with more frequent feedback loops. Prototyping is an essential part of the build and test portions of the learning cycle structure—plan, design, build, test, review results. Organizations know how to do development, but a key to innovative lean development is the elimination of wastes, and increased speed in development.

Rapid prototyping—quickly making representative models of the ideas for evaluation and review—does both. Early in the development process, teams have less confidence in their ideas and there are more ideas to consider. In some fashion, all of these ideas must be prototyped to either prove or disprove the feasibility of each one. Whether for a customer validation or a management review, there has to be a version available for audience reaction so that its feedback can help the development team better frame the project goals, and make the connections between wants and possible solutions. This gives constant, real-time feedback for possible course correction.

Imagine, for example, that a customer wants something like a water bottle, but has not described it clearly. The spoken want is a container to hold liquid. If the development team assumes that it already knows just what the customer wants and proceeds down the path of developing something like a coffee mug, it will have satisfied the spoken want, but not provided a solution to the unspoken wants. The customer will not be satisfied, and the development team will have to do quite a bit of rework to satisfy the real, but unspoken, wants.

Suppose instead that the same development team quickly came back to the customer with a sketch of the coffee mug, along with some sketches of other possibilities. The reaction would help steer them toward the true vision. For example, at the first validation the response might be, "No, it cannot have a handle." Immediately, all mug-looking solutions are out. From reviewing and discussing all of the proposed possibilities, the development team and customer are able to move toward a round container without a handle. After the next learning cycle, the team shows a few versions of ceramic, plastic, and glass cups. The customer reaction is, "I like the round ones, but it cannot be glass for safety reasons—and can you make it transparent?" Off the team goes to develop and prototype further.

As the learning cycles continue, the feedback keeps shaping the result. The team makes more prototypes and eventually discovers all of the true requirements: a solution that fits into existing holders, is resealable and recyclable, and has a company logo on it. As the ideas become more refined, the prototypes take on more sophistication, and each round of feedback is even more valuable. In the end, the customer requirements for the water bottle are satisfied, and the development team has designed a successful product.

What happened to achieve this result?

- The project team realized the customer was the ultimate authority on wants, and worked to clarify and extract these as development took place. Discussion helped, but without the prototypes, the team could not have fully met the customer's needs.
- Early and regular idea refinement allowed modifications to be made early, thereby avoiding major rework, minimizing costs, and maximizing the possibility of meeting the schedule.
- Working backward from flawless execution, the design freeze could be at the latest possible date, allowing maximum freedom for product changes without jeopardizing the project schedule.

Rapid prototyping is an essential part of innovative lean development. It applies to products, services, and software. An IBM study found that:

- 55% of application development projects go over budget.
- 68% of application development projects exceed schedule.
- 88% of application development projects require a major redesign.

Sound familiar? That is some major league waste. With rapid prototyping, innovative lean development practitioners aim to shape the development direction early and often to provide a solution to spoken customer wants while simultaneously avoiding missing the mark by not fulfilling the unspoken wants.

Development is about creating a profitable value stream for the company. To accomplish that, development teams must play by their own company rules for timing and profitability, but they must also repeatedly validate with customers so the customers get what they want, when they need it—unspoken wants and all.

Learning cycles also call for user validation within each learning cycle. This means that in every single learning cycle, the future users of the system are brought in to review the progress with the team. In the earliest learning cycles, this is done by drawing process maps (preferably value stream maps) with the user to understand their process. In this way, the IT team can learn the actual process the users use on a day-to-day basis to accomplish their work. By focusing on the process maps, the IT team can also start thinking about a future state, the optimum and most efficient method for the process. In later learning cycles, users can be shown out-of-the-box capabilities or base functionalities. All of these are forms of prototyping during a learning cycle.

In other words, it shows the user what the basic software can do, without all of the added automation and features that will eventually be included in the system. If these are not intuitive to the users, storyboarding or images of screen shots may need to be shown to them as well. The idea is to get early feedback on the software before a lot of effort is placed into writing program code.

As the learning cycles progress and the system develops, users can continue to give feedback. Bringing the users in early is very important because it dramatically increases the quality and efficiency of the final system. In addition, users should be brought into the learning cycle on a regular and frequent schedule. They should not be brought in only at the close of a learning cycle merely to review what the IT team has accomplished. At a minimum, for a 3- to 4-week learning cycle, users should be brought in every week. There is a tremendous side benefit to doing this because the training needs of the users can be captured and defined as the system enfolds. User involvement can shave a large amount of time off the development cycle.

Teams practicing lean development have made tremendous strides in this arena in IT and product development. By utilizing these prototyping and validating methods, they have seen the overall schedule reduced by half, greatly reduced rework, and reduced user training. Rapid prototyping, along with validation, work to converge on an innovation solution much earlier than conventional approaches would.

The Value of Using Multiple Prototyping Techniques

Almost all projects have a deadline, and the project team is going to need every advantage to accomplish it. Prototypes should reflect the level of the solution. Early in the project, the team is carrying multiple unproven concepts forward, which is the idea of set-based design.

The innovative lean development method merges the concept of set-based design with learning cycles and prototyping. The learning cycles help to quickly narrow the concepts to the one or two that best fit the customer's requirements. The learning cycles provide a structure for the teams to reach their goals. Prototyping within each learning cycle helps to reduce the risks by proving out solutions with actual physical models.

These visual models can be sketches, foam-core models, rough "works-like" models, computer simulations finite element analysis (FEA), mechanism design, mathematical optimizations, and so on, and more finished "looks-like" models. As the project progresses, subsystems should be brought together to see how they fit, and finally the entire system level build can take place, validating the fit of these separate elements (see Figure 7.1).

Physical models are leveraged because they can teach the team so much more than electronic computer-assisted design (CAD) models. In the earliest learning cycles, sketches, drawings, and even CAD models are the

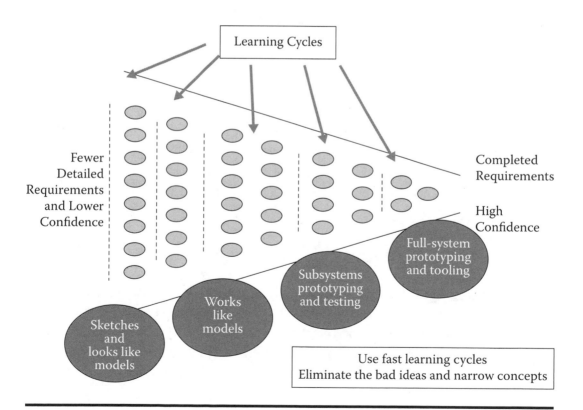

Figure 7.1   Product prototype concepts narrowed in learning cycles.

only representations of the design. However, the team must quickly create actual models of the product to make the ideas readily understood by the customer.

Architects use this technique extensively to gather requirements and validate them with the client as early as the concept phase because not everyone is able to make the leap from drawings of a building to an image of what the building will actually look like. Architects use small-scale 3D models of the structure to show the client what the design will look like once built. The models are a form of validation.

In each learning cycle the opportunity exists to prototype to help answer the various questions presented in that learning cycle, and prototyping should be thought of as the method by which to gain the answers to these questions. Carefully worded objectives and questions will lead the team to build the prototypes to answer the questions.

> *By using the innovative lean development method to refine the objectives and prototype them during learning cycles, confidence in the solutions will increase dramatically.*

Each learning cycle must have an element of prototyping. If the product is a physical object, the prototype should be a physical, testable item. However, the technique can be extended to other things such as processes or services. Even IT systems can benefit dramatically from prototyping.

In IT systems, the prototypes are screen shots, sample programs to test key development concepts, and finally working subsystems with real coding. The innovative lean development method requires that the prototypes be subparts of the whole and that they are actually tested (see Figure 7.2).

How to Test Prototypes

In the learning cycle lexicon, prototypes are the build part of the cycle, but the teams must also test these models. Prototypes are essential for showing the concepts developed by the team. In each learning cycle, the development team needs to design and build the tests that will be done on the prototypes. These tests can take many forms, and they will evolve through the life of the project.

Just as in building, the prototypes should match the level of the project phase, the testing of these prototypes needs to match the sophistication of

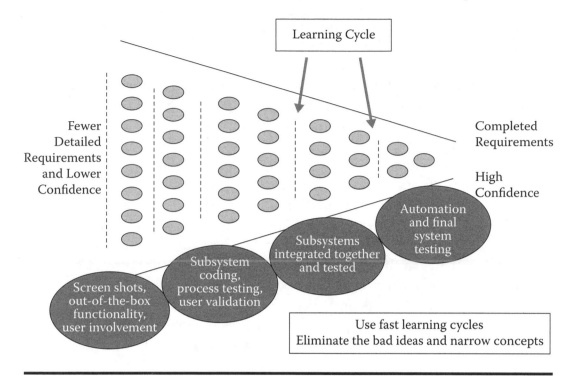

Figure 7.2   IT prototype concepts narrowed through learning cycles.

the project at that time. Initial testing shows the early concepts to stakeholders to obtain feedback and to connect the customer to the vision. Going forward, internal testing needs to escalate.

As development progresses, evaluation could include:

- *Equations:* Showing how the team expects the model to work, perhaps in ideal conditions.
- *Models:* Rough or more finished, in sketch or CAD format, models can show size and scope and can reveal such things as assembly time or possible installation problems. Especially early in a project, models are the most powerful type of evaluation.
- *Historical Review:* As discussed in Chapter 2, hindsight is a ready reminder of what has—and has not—worked in the history of this and other situations. Don't dismiss ideas because "we haven't done it that way before"; history can help guide the team to converge on a solution.
- *Simulations:* Use structure finite element analysis on parts and systems; try a database with a select user group; test a subsystem of the new

planning software with experienced designers; let a small group of internal users try a development run of the new product; such simulations feed better development.

- *Physical Tests:* As the project matures and physical prototypes are produced, physical tests are required. Industry standards may apply or a company may have stringent testing requirements; regardless, for best results, involve all the stakeholders. Be clear that the suppliers know what kinds of tests are needed. This might be the most overlooked area for increased innovation and avoiding rework. Seek out experts from the supply chain and use their input in the development process.

- *Measure Concepts against Requirements:* As a constant reminder of what the development team is trying to accomplish, regularly and religiously match the concepts carried forward with the project requirements. If a gap starts to develop between these, the earlier it is identified, the better. Management plays a crucial role here.

- *Customer Validation:* In innovative lean development, customer validation is required. Testing the concepts against the customer wants uncovers both customer reaction and the unspoken customer wants.

- *Prototypes and Testing of those Prototypes:* The crucial build and test components of the innovative lean development learning cycle minimize project risks. The goal is knowledge and communication. Therefore, the sooner the situation is known and communicated to stakeholders the sooner a solution can be put into place.

Case Study: Prototyping and Testing for Each Learning Cycle

The goal is to build some speed in development with rapid, iterative prototyping. Show stakeholders how something might look, rather than exactly how it will look.

Suppose the product idea and marketing direction are to create a new metal shelf to hold 40 pounds of books, papers, or any other objects. Based on the experience of the team and the project deadlines, the new shelf needs to be developed in just five short learning cycles, which could range in length from 2 to 4 weeks. The goal of each learning cycle is to answer specific development questions. Here is how the learning cycles might be organized and a description of what might happen in each learning cycle.

Learning Cycle 1

The first learning cycle objectives involve choosing a material and processing technique. The questions could be:

- What should the material be?
- What are the test requirements?
- How will dislodgement from the panel be prevented?

At this stage, the development team should consider any material from plastic to steel to aluminum for the shelf itself. All of the marketing product features are set out in a formal document that, while detailed, may not completely define all the requirements. There needs to be discussion about what the final colors will be (the team will have some initial thoughts about colors), and no thought yet is given to how labels would be added to the shelf. In the first learning cycle scope document, the team should add an objective to select a color palette that would coordinate with the other products in the line and another to further define the labeling for the shelf.

In the first learning cycle, the innovative lean development method calls for the generation of multiple concepts. Here the design team should look outside the company, by contracting with several outside firms to generate concepts. Each could be funded for a specific amount of time and given the mission to come up with several viable sources within the framework of the first learning cycle. Although the team may not yet create physical prototypes, the sketches (as shown in Figure 7.3) and CAD models developed

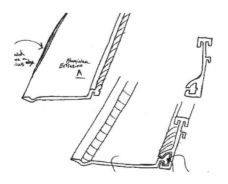

1
Multiple Conceptual Sketches

Figure 7.3   Learning cycle 1.

by the outside firms and internal designers can act as the prototypes for the team. The concepts developed become the input for the next learning cycle.

Learning Cycle 2

In the next learning cycle, the team might define the performance of the materials based on the designs submitted by the outside firms.

In this learning cycle, simple cardboard models of the shelf and dividers are built. From the prototypes, marketing and engineering can discover that the shelf dimension should be a little deeper to accommodate a variety of books and binders. During the learning cycle, the team should also prototype the first concepts for a label holder for the front edge of the shelf. Prototype CAD models can show how the parts might come together.

One of the key objectives in the second learning cycle might involve picking the final material for the shelf and determining the maximum proof load that the shelf should carry. As pictured in Figure 7.4, a trade-off curve between the materials shows the performance (deflection) of the shelf under increased load for different sizes. Aluminum shows the best performance characteristics and it best matches the rest of the product line. The aluminum extrusion supplier should be brought into the learning cycle to provide input about the design and its manufacturability.

The whole process is a discovery and learning process. The aluminum extrusion supplier would indicate that the cross-section profile of the entire

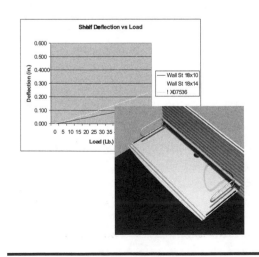

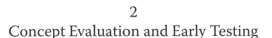

2
Concept Evaluation and Early Testing

Figure 7.4   Learning cycle 2.

shelf is too wide for most aluminum extrusion presses. In fact, the extruder explains that they know of only two locations in the country that operate a press large enough to extrude the shelf in one piece. Now the team has to scramble, but that is the value of learning cycles—quick learning and adjustments to solve the problem.

Using outsight to solve the problem, the team looks around to other products and processes, and they discover that most large extruded objects are seamed in some way. This discovery leads them to ask the supplier a series of questions:

- Can two sections of aluminum extrusions be seamed together but still provide a solid connection?
- How large a cross-section profile can be extruded by most aluminum extrusion presses?
- Can the profiles imagined be built in the tool?
- How would the two pieces be assembled together?

These questions are added to the learning cycle scope document, and the team starts searching for the answers.

As they receive answers to their questions from the supplier, they discover that the supplier already has a design for connecting two pieces of aluminum on a corner seam. However, the technique had not yet been attempted for a flat section seamed together in the center. The learning objective for the next learning cycle will be to examine concepts to seam two flat extrusions together.

Learning Cycle 3

In learning cycle 3, the team works on a very simple prototype to test the technique of placing a seam down the center of the shelf, parallel to the front edge, as shown in Figure 7.5. The prototype shows the scale of the profile that will be needed. The intent is to keep the profile on the bottom of the shelf, and to keep it as small as possible. The prototype models allowed the team to understand how the profile will function.

The team becomes concerned that the market might not accept a seam. The primary market for the product is especially sensitive to any place that might collect dirt and germs, and the seam might be a collection spot. The marketing member of the team validates this with the field. As a result, the team decides to finish the parts after assembly, instead of before assembly.

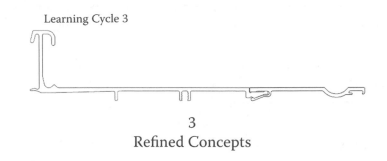

Learning Cycle 3

3
Refined Concepts

Figure 7.5   Learning cycle 3.

This seemingly simple refinement to the requirements actually presents quite a challenge. Now the joint has to be rigid enough to ensure that the finish coat will not crack or chip. More discoveries and more refinement to the design are needed in the next learning cycle surrounding these new findings.

Learning Cycle 4

In the fourth learning cycle, the team refines the hypothesis that they could create a completely rigid joint between the two sections of extrusions depicted in Figure 7.6. This innovative approach is based on the outsight that other products manufactured by the supplier have rigid corner seams.

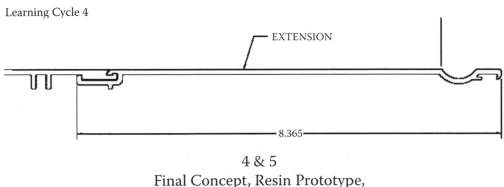

Learning Cycle 4

EXTENSION

8.365

4 & 5
Final Concept, Resin Prototype,
Final Prototype Extrusion Die

Figure 7.6   Learning cycles 4 and 5.

The Rule of Outsight: typically, the whole design is not imported; instead, the innovator imports the portion of the idea that applies to the new situation.

The team imports the idea of the seam between two sections of the extrusion; however, it still needs to adapt the idea to its own shelf design.

Next, the team tests the profile prior to cutting the actual extrusion die. They decide to cut the profile in resin, which allows them to quickly validate the seam in the fourth learning cycle. The resin prototype allows them to prove out their concept for the interlocking seam.

Learning Cycle 5

In the fifth learning cycle, the team actually has two aluminum extrusion dies built, one for the front section of the shelf and one for the back section of the shelf. The careful thinking and prototyping in the previous four learning cycles has led to a functioning set of extrusion dies that not only create products for testing, but also yield tools that can be used to create products for a trade show. The prototypes might be usable in the initial production runs as well. The plastic extrusions for the label generation also are built in this learning cycle.

The result of using learning cycles helped the team achieve its goals.

- The team increased the knowledge about the product and process much earlier, and this helped the team produce a design integrated into the value stream.
- By bringing the supplier into the process, costs were known earlier, and discoveries (outsights) for design were proven out in the very early learning cycles.
- By informing management of the learning at the end of each learning cycle, integrated management decision making was achieved.
- Flow interrupters were held off and considered at the start of the next learning cycle, which allowed the learning cycles to finish on time.
- The quality of the design compared to similar products in the marketplace increased, making it more functional and competitive.

Overall, the conclusion is that an innovative lean development method has a higher quality output that meets the needs of the customer, and the output is achieved sooner. Both the customer and the supply chain are brought into the process earlier to achieve insights that would not otherwise be found. The output of the process takes into consideration how various wastes in the production process can be avoided. In all these ways, innovative lean development removes wastes that then never get into the production process for the final solution. The method also values the knowledge gained during learning cycles as much as the solution itself. The knowledge becomes an important building block for the projects that follow in the footsteps of the current project.

Chapter 8

How to Apply Lean Management Principles to Innovation

"Management works in the system; leadership works on the system."

Stephen R. Covey, author and management expert

A fair amount of ground has been covered in the quest to describe a system for companies that wish to implement innovative lean development, and many important principles that are critical to the creation of a new innovative lean development system were discussed including how to:

- Identify the value of a product, process, or service from a customer's perspective
- Create designs that are lean from the start by eliminating waste from the system
- Create customer value by pulling the needs of the customer into creating the values
- Validate both the value statement and the prototypes created during the learning cycles

All of these concepts fit with the lean philosophy as implemented in lean manufacturing around the world. The final capstone in any lean architecture is the most important; it is to strive for perfection and to seek continuous improvement. Continuous improvement is the area in which leadership is especially important.

Lean leadership in innovative lean development is critical to transforming the organizational culture. The practice of applying leader standard work and leader-led gemba walks are completely transparent (i.e., transferable) from lean manufacturing, to the lean office, and to the lean development process. In fact, gemba methods and tools can be adapted to a lean system that will sustain an innovative lean development initiative in any organization. To summarize:

- Lean is an improvement system. At its core, lean thinking means we are always seeking improvement. We are never finished improving the way we develop or the methods that we use.
- Lean is a journey. Once you take the first step toward a more innovative and lean development process, you never actually arrive. The organization and its members will always be striving for perfection.

The Function of Lean Management of Innovative Lean Development

Think of the lean journey as a journey by rail. On the tracks, there are two rails and the ties that hold them together. The first rail includes the physical and technical changes required for a conversion to lean development: a redefinition of value, elimination of waste, predictive measuring, and idea generation that focuses on placing that company's design above its competition's.

The second and less obvious rail is the change in the way development is managed, focusing more on the process, relying more on visual controls, and creating pace in development through short learning cycles focused on specific goals. The new management focus requires learning the importance of sticking to a defined process and making it standard throughout the organization—a technique that is defined as standard work in the lean lexicon.

The third component—the ties that keep the two rails together—is a change in thinking. It is the most difficult to achieve. It requires imposing the same kind of disciplined adherence to process on those in leadership positions as those leaders demand of the development teams they instruct and inspire to work in new ways. It requires paying attention to process on at least the same level as is paid to achieving results.

The technical side of lean isn't hard to understand or even to implement. Successful conversions to lean manufacturing demonstrate that less than 20% of the work involves designing and making the physical changes. By far the greater effort, time, and struggle are in changing the way leaders think and altering their approach to day-to-day management. At an AME conference presentation, the president of Toyota spoke about the successful lean program at his company. He called the Toyota Production System the Thinking Production System, noting that it requires a change in behavior in order to change the culture.

An informal survey of practitioners of lean in manufacturing revealed that changes to the production environment have only a 30% success rate. In other words, 70% of lean implementations experience decay and a return to the original way of doing business. Many lean practitioners have notable early failures to show for their initial effort. To change a development culture to be both lean and innovative is just as difficult.

Traditional batch and queue development and innovative lean development have significant differences. We have all heard demands for performance, "Don't tell me what you have to do to get it done, just get the results!" Getting results is the focus of business; it is part of the DNA of most businesses. In fact, many companies search for results-oriented managers, because leaders know that they will make things happen.

Focus on Process to Create Innovative Lean Development

A results orientation is good. However, to get results, innovative lean development focuses on process to search for the proper value definition and the early identification of potential wastes. Once discovered, innovative tools are applied to create new solutions and ideas that are rapidly iterated upon using learning cycles.

The key to sustaining innovative lean development systems is to focus on the process. In fact, when every instinct and habit of the organization shouts out, "Results, Results, RESULTS!" the lean thinking development leader has to respond, "No! Process, Process, PROCESS!"

Innovative lean development is all about process, and lean management closes the loop on process discipline. The lean thinking development leader's mantra begins with the leader standard work, which calls for visual controls and daily accountability to sustain and improve the development efforts throughout learning cycles. It also calls for team members to capture knowledge generated during the process, and for the whole organization to become a learning organization.

> *A Different Perspective: lean thinkers search out problems where none is thought to exist and work to eliminate their causes.*

Traditional development thinking focuses on results. The system as a whole might be robust, but its elements are unstable, prone to repeated problems, full of waiting, workarounds, rework, wasted time, overworked people, and idiosyncratic processes that optimize one part at the expense of others. Batch systems produce results, but not without many kinds of extra costs. Even carefully constructed project schedules are fraught with problems, and they are immediately out of date. The inherent reason all project schedules are mistrusted as soon as they are drafted is that, when dealing with a heuristic process, discoveries cannot be predicted using complex project schedules.

Innovative lean development focuses on a process that enables and encourages discovery at a faster pace. The system is robust, finely tuned, and interdependent, with minimum overhead required from the team and project managers. Process problems will show up right away in each learning cycle, and they have to be addressed by leadership to keep the system functioning. Lean systems are more efficient, but they do require higher maintenance than batch systems.

In the traditional development world, "doing whatever it takes" is a point of pride. In lean systems, consistent performance demands root cause value and waste definitions rather than workarounds. The idea is to take care of the process so that the process will make leadership and management easier and more effective.

How to Change the Development Culture

Implementing innovative lean development does nothing to change the management system. A conventional batch-based development system will keep huffing and puffing along unless some action is taken to change it. During the changeover to learning cycles and more systematic innovation techniques, leadership will also have to take action to change the management system.

This means addressing virtually every aspect of a development manager's role, with the exception of the manager's skills in dealing with people. As a manager converts to lean, some things have to start over.

The challenge lies in changing the thinking of the managers in the development system. One senior leader put it this way, "Leaders and their people do not see their responsibility as being part of a process. People are not measured this way in their performance appraisals, and may not be paid to think this way, either." The way to increase the chances of innovative lean development taking root and blossoming in an organization is to set up a vertically aligned program from scenario management, to the leaders, to the staff.

The whole organization has to move to a culture that involves more learning and knowledge capture. Everyone has to be asked to think in this new way. The process needs to change from one that collects batch requirements to one that continually refines requirements and solutions through prototyping during learning cycles. The staff has to be encouraged and expected to use learning cycles to enable discovery. The lean thinking development leader also has to expect the whole organization to think in innovative ways. Instead of saying, "Show me the results," a lean thinking development leader should say, "Show me the wastebasket and failures."

Over time, with the leaders asking for change, the development culture will change.

What Is Work Culture and How to Change It

In the language of social science, *culture* is a hypothetical construct, which is a fancy way of saying it is an idea devised to make sense of and organize a group's experiences. Culture, therefore, arises from what is seen, but it is an idea that is created in the mind, an inference. Similarly, work culture is actually the sum of habits among members of a work group. It is "the way things are done around here."

In terms of innovative lean development, the question is, "How do you get a handle on it; how do you change culture?" and the answer is, "Culture is not changed directly." To alter a culture, the people in the culture must

Figure 8.1   Targets for changing the development culture.

change their day-to-day behavior. The object of cultural change is not the culture itself; it is the behavior of the people.

To convert to an innovative lean development culture, three areas must be targeted for change: practices, behaviors, and habits.

These attributes (see Figure 8.1) are the things that are seen and experienced, things that can be directly changed and influenced. That is what a lean management system is all about: changing the attributes of practices, behaviors, and habits.

To change a culture, old habitual behaviors must be replaced with new ones. The good news for lean thinking development leaders is that new practices, behaviors, and habits can become the norm when leaders make expectations clear and follow up with the development teams.

The way to change a habit is to replace the old habit with a new one that is incompatible with the old.*

---

* David Mann. *Creating a Lean Culture*, p. 16.

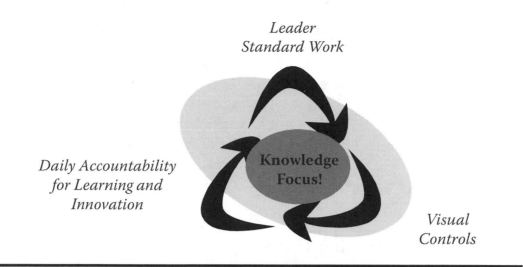

Figure 8.2 The foundations of lean management.

A way to promote the capture of knowledge is to require that it be mandatory to do so at the end of every learning cycle. If the team does this regularly, it will become a practice.

The lean thinking leader's goal is to establish new expectations of the development team that modify their practices, behaviors, and habits.

Visual controls are fundamental to communicating the status of the project to the leader (and to the rest of the team). By establishing the expectation that the development team will use a visual tracking system, the leader will help the team display the status of the current learning cycle on a daily basis.

If the visual controls are the "what" of the lean thinking leadership system, then the leader standard work is the "how" of the way that leaders goes about their work. The purpose of leader standard work is to discipline the leader to follow the same process each week and thereby set a clear example for the team of what is expected.

Leader Standard Work

There are four dimensions of leader standard work in the innovative lean development system:

1. Standards for learning cycles
2. Standards for innovation
3. Standards for visual controls
4. Standards for knowledge capture

For each standard, there are diagnostic questions that will help the leader know what to ask when interacting with the team. The standards also offer a way for the leader to objectively rate the team on how well it is following the lean development system.

Standards for Learning Cycles

In the case of the learning cycles, the questions are designed to help the team maximize the learning or problem-solving activities. Each learning objective should have multiple, unanswered questions that are linked to tasks that are owned by individuals on the team. The questions should also be designed to determine if the objective is stated clearly so that true design trade-offs will be generated during the learning cycle. The questions should also encourage innovation by asking the team if multiple concepts have been considered as potential solution sets for the learning objective.

Lean Management Standards—Diagnostic Questions for Learning Cycles
1. Will the block plan's overall objectives produce the deliverables of this phase of the project on time?
2. What are the team's knowledge capture practices?
3. Are learning cycle questions specific, linked to objectives, and owned by individuals?
4. To what degree will answering the learning cycle questions address learning cycle objectives?
5. Does the scope document govern the content and activities of the learning cycle?
6. Do the objectives create a contrast between competing criteria and expose a knowledge gap that applies to this project and is applicable to future projects?
7. Will the team meet the short-term schedule for this learning cycle?
8. Have parallel multiple concepts been developed in this learning cycle, or are multiple concepts being comparatively evaluated in this learning cycle?

Standards for Innovation

In the case of innovation, the development leader should encourage the team members to assess how deeply their innovation efforts penetrate into uncharted waters. The leader should be asking questions about both the quantity and the quality of those ideas and should be seeking to determine with the team if the ideas link back to the original value and waste definitions as well as to whether they link back to the four domains of innovative solutions.

Lean Management Standards—Diagnostic Questions for Innovation

1. Is there evidence that the team is generating innovative ideas?

2. How many ideas from nonrelated industries or from nature has the team explored?

3. What ideas has the team rejected and has the team developed multiple solution sets? Is the focus on both short-term and long-term innovation?

4. Has the team rated concepts against the attributes (values) and lean wastes (is it lean from the start)?

5. Has the team linked project ideas to corporate strategy and user-centered research?

6. How wide is the application of the innovation across product, process, supply chain, and customers?

7. How integrated is innovation and learning cycles?

In the case of the visual controls and accountability, the leader should be encouraging the team members to look at the pace of the learning cycles. The questions should help to assess how well the tasks map to the learning objectives and questions. This should also be an opportunity to balance the workload (another lean concept) across the team. This is very exciting because the team will see, through the mapping of tasks on a daily basis, where the bulk of the work lands, and who has too much work and who does not have enough. This gives the leader a chance to balance resources dynamically across multiple subteams by reassigning existing team members or calling in additional people as needed. The leader should also ask questions to determine how closely the team is following the lean process. In other words, is the team practicing the new habits that the new lean process requires?

Standard work for the team meetings themselves is the cement that will hold the meetings together. Regular accountability meetings are meant to be short and to the point. Anything over 15 minutes is too long. These sessions are not problem-solving sessions; they are update and discovery sessions.

Standards for Visual Controls

A standard tool in lean thinking is establishing visual controls. In development, visual control boards may meet with great resistance. Without visual controls, however, there is no accountability, and no big picture for assessing how the project is going. Visual controls are not optional in innovative lean development. In the example of the visual control board, the leader's standard work would be to regularly follow up, probably weekly, to review the accuracy and completeness of the information posted to the visual board.

How to Manage Team Activities with Accountability Boards

Team accountability is helpful to team members and management in determining where work may be piling up, uncovering an otherwise invisible bottleneck, and so on. Accountability boards are one type of visual control. They can help balance workloads of teams as they work to increase speed in development.

How to Track Flow Interrupters and Log Issues

Occasionally, work cannot progress due to something out of the team's control. This is a flow interrupter and must be elevated to management for immediate resolution. If there is nothing tracked or logged when such issues arise, management has no visibility and cannot help.

How to Facilitate Communication within the Team and with Management

Lean principles are best used as an effective communication tool. To keep projects on track, the team must be aware of the problems and potential problems it might encounter. The principle is for the team to communicate frequently, thus maintaining the pace during the development effort.

How to Utilize Visual Controls

Development team members are a collection of experts, each with specialized skills and knowledge, and each one brings unique skills and perspectives to the team. The members of the team may also return to their departments with things on their to-do lists. The challenge lies in maintaining a rapid pace of activity toward the development goals with a diverse and sometimes dispersed team.

When the team is physically located in the same area, a visual control board is the most effective method for sharing project information and tasks. Visual control boards are used throughout a lean manufacturing facility to ensure projects are tracking to completion and tasks are accomplished. Making the board visible ensures that the information is persistent. When a

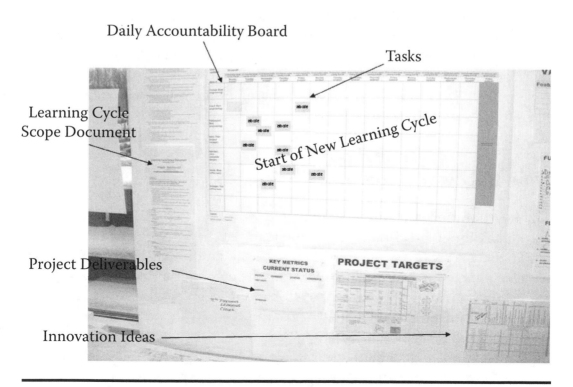

Figure 8.3   Visual control board for development.

board is visible and displayed in the team area the whole team can tell at a glance what the project status is at that point in time. It also provides a very good place for management to take a gemba walk.

A visual control board provides a vehicle to bring the team together on a frequent and regular basis. Teams should meet multiple times per week at the visual control boards. The meetings provide a vehicle to talk about progress, discuss flow interrupters, and review items learned.

Visual controls should always be customized for the team. No two visual controls need to be alike. However, it is advisable to standardize the visual control board as much as possible. Standardization allows team members and management to move seamlessly between groups without confusion, retraining, or loss of efficiency. High-performance teams gain success by using the boards daily to track progress, tasks, and issues.

Several important documents should be posted on the board. The learning cycle scope document describes what the team is seeking to accomplish in the current learning cycle. The scope document records the objectives and questions to be answered in the learning cycle. Even if this document exists electronically, it will be available for ready reference when it is posted to the visual display board.

Key project deliverables help steer the team in the right direction. The visual board is also the place to capture these project deliverables. Metrics to consider capturing are the project's end target and the capital and expense numbers. The main project values, or statement of work, can be displayed here as well. In addition, the ideas emanating from an innovation brainstorming session should be captured on the visual board.

How to Utilize Accountability Boards

The heart of the board is the accountability board, often called the daily accountability board. This is where the team meets on a regular basis, preferably daily, to go over the tasks that it is working on to achieve the learning cycle objectives and answer the questions. The correct format is to list the names of the team members in the left-hand margin and the dates across the top. Each team member should post the tasks to support the learning objectives and questions.

To measure the pace of the learning cycle, multiple tasks for each question are required to chart the progress being made toward the answer. The team should avoid placing only the tasks' deadlines on the board because this does not allow the team to predict whether the activity is on track to meet that deadline.

It is common to use green and red dots to indicate whether a task is complete or late:

- If a task is completed on time, it gets a green dot.
- If a task is not complete, it gets a red dot.
- The second day a task is late, it gets another red dot.
- For each day the task is late, another red dot is added.
- Tasks with red dots receive a green dot when completed.

As a rule, the due date for a task is never changed. Moving the date a task is due sends a message that the deadline is unimportant, and, when a task is moved, the original due date is lost. Instead of moving the tasks, they are marked with a red dot. Most teams feel comfortable with this system within a few days, but a strong team leader to facilitate the sessions is very helpful.

There are several benefits to the visual accountability boards. The boards help the team balance the tasks among the resources on the team. When one member's tasks are all due on a given date, the other team members will quickly notice this and will have an opportunity to help offload some of the work. In addition, if a team member goes red on a task, there usually is a good reason for the miss, one that is outside of the member's control. A red dot is a process miss, and a process miss is an opportunity for the team and its leader to recover by addressing the root cause problem.

Tracking Flow Interrupters and Log Issues

If a task is marked with several red dots, it is time for the team to assess why it is late. Remember, there generally is an external reason for multiple misses, rather than a problem associated with the person who was assigned the task. These are the flow interrupters. Flow interrupters should be logged on the board, and owners should be assigned to resolve the problem. When flow interrupters hit the team, it is a chance for the leadership to get involved and help remove the roadblocks or apply different resources.

Visual controls are an extremely powerful tool to manage the pace of the learning cycle. Physical visual controls are more powerful than electronic versions, but both have been used with success. Either type, when used properly, will help the team to prioritize its work and maintain the pace of the project.

Lean Management Standards—Diagnostic Questions for Visual Controls and Accountability

1. Are tasks visible, and do they support the questions and objectives of the learning cycle?

2. Do visual controls coordinate/balance workloads, show pace and progression of work?

3. Are reasons for flow interrupters described clearly enough to decide what next steps to take and are next steps assigned owners along with due dates?

4. Are visuals regularly reviewed by the team?

5. Are visuals regularly reviewed by leaders in the area? Do regular gemba walks take place?

6. Is there standard work for the meeting and legends for the visual tools?

Standards for Knowledge Capture

The lean leader should encourage the team to create the habit and practice of capturing the knowledge learned during each cycle. The development leader should expect the answers to questions to be captured and stored. If the company does not yet have a formal system for capturing the knowledge, the leader must ensure that the location is known and well documented for future reference.

The goal is to ensure that the knowledge can be used by other teams for other design problems by documenting them in such a way as to be useful in the future. Encourage the team to adopt a publish mentality for their peers. When knowledge is shared openly and freely across and between various disciplines, the organization has the opportunity to leverage all of the information by applying it in multiple settings.

Lean Management Standards—Diagnostic Questions for Knowledge Capture
1. Are answers to learning cycle questions being documented, and, if so, how are they being documented?
2. What has the team learned?
3. What are the general issues?
4. Have the knowledge gap questions been captured in a standard format and stored to a central location?
5. Have the knowledge gap answers been framed in a way that can be applied to this and future situations?

Lean Management Diagnostic Tool

The lean management standard also provides a diagnostic tool to rate the team on each of the four dimensions. The team can rate itself, and the leader can rate the team. The standard is to rate the team on a scale ranging from just starting out to fully sustaining the innovative lean development implementation. The goal is for the lean thinking leader and the team to understand how well they are progressing on the journey to a new culture of innovative lean development.

Rating	Description
Pre-implementation	Team is just starting out, there is little evidence of improved processes and new habits, and the team is just learning the new innovative lean development process.
Beginning implementation	The team is starting to show new behavior and habits, but the team requires a fair amount of coaching and mentoring.
First recognizable state	The team is demonstrating the new behaviors and habits, but it requires ongoing coaching from the leader.
System stabilizing	The team is beginning to be self-sustaining. They might require some coaching and follow-up from the leader.
System sustaining	The team is self-governing. It performs self-assessments and grades on how well it is following the new process.

How to Assess the Standards

To illustrate how to assess the standards, consider visual controls and accountability for an ongoing IT development project. The team is working at implementing the standards and learning as it goes. To evaluate the completeness and accuracy of the visual board, use the diagnostic questions for visual controls to assess where the team currently stands against the standard. The goal of the assessment is to point out opportunities for improvement. The results are not a grade but an evaluation of the current innovative lean development journey.

1. Are tasks visible and do they support the questions and objectives of the learning cycle?

The answer is "yes" if the visual board is populated with numerous tasks, which are linked back to the questions and objectives of the learning cycle.

2. Do visual controls coordinate/balance workloads and show pace and progression of work?

The answer is "yes" if the tasks are shared among the team members so that the deadlines are met. Note: the visual board should also indicate vacations or other time away from the office for each team member. Thus, there also will be evidence that team members are covering for their peers who are out of the office to ensure that the learning cycle is progressing at the intended pace.

3. Are reasons for flow interrupters described clearly enough to decide on the next steps, and are owners assigned to the next steps along with due dates?

Look for a place on the board where issues are logged and managed. Even if the list of issues and flow interrupters exists in an electronic database located elsewhere, evidence of the top issues should appear on the board, with their owners identified and due dates assigned.

4. Are visuals regularly reviewed by the team?

Examine the board for recent updates and current information. A board that has not been used for a week indicates the start of the decay in adherence to the process.

5. Are visuals reviewed regularly by leaders in the area, and do regular gemba walks take place?

The evidence cannot always be discerned by looking at the board, but the team leader should have a standard work checklist as a reminder of when to check the board regularly. The leader should be keeping notes on the standard work documenting what was seen on the board, along with areas of potential improvement.

6. Is there standard work for the meeting, and are there legends for the visual tools?

Search the board for legends indicating what the symbols and lettering means. A documented standard agenda that the team uses every time it meets at the board should be available.

Again, the evaluation is a look at the lean development journey as it is happening. The gemba walk provides a snapshot of the journey, but it does not provide a map of the full lean voyage.

Gemba walking—one of the tools used by the lean leader—is a way for the leader to engage with an ongoing project to foster improvement. There is no substitute for this involvement. The leader should be making adjustments and looking for evidence of progress that indicate that the lean development practice and culture is advancing. As one leader described it, "I prefer to catch a team doing the right thing. This is much better than always telling them that they are not doing the right things."

Self-evaluation is a tool that a leader uses to look at the process from a different direction. Evaluation of an area by company leadership quickly enables direction and ownership. By using open-ended questions, leaders can determine the status of lean development within a team and, more important, generate ideas for improvement. As the ideas for enhancement emerge, the leader will have a clearer idea of where to start, what to work on, and how to proceed.

Consider this guide for rating the development and improvement:

Innovative Lean Development Assessment
1–2 = No visible evidence of this practice
3–4 = Occasional evidence found
5–6 = Practiced in some areas
7–8 = Practiced in most areas
9–10 = Consistently practiced throughout the organization

Again, the beauty of this approach is that it evaluates not only direction, but it builds ownership of that direction in both the leadership and the team. The assessment should never be given to the team without ideas on how to improve the process. As we have seen, ideas are the engine for a better process, faster development, and more innovation.

Start Now and Put Innovative Lean Development to Work

Innovative lean development is good business. Development is the heart of your organization. Innovation is the differentiator for your products. Applying lean principles to development provides direction, feedback, and adjustment, resulting in reduced waste and increased speed. Keep at it and the desired cultural shift toward a learning organization will occur.

The plans, tools, templates, and examples in this book are based on the experiences of the authors, both of whom have seen teams make great strides forward and a few stumbles along the way. As with any journey toward excellence, there is no end to this process, but there must be a beginning. Leaders and project managers should work toward establishing several behaviors and practices in teams. Consider using this seven-step process to launch the first team.

1. Train a pilot team in the concepts of innovative lean development.
2. Build a project block plan of the learning cycles, working backward from the point of flawless execution.

3. Establish targets and measures of success, including the innovation gaps that must be closed by the team.
4. Implement learning cycles to close the gap. Appendix A outlines the framework to get started.
5. Create visual controls and accountability to ensure that the pace of the learning cycles is maintained.
6. Schedule and lead regular status meetings, setting the pitch for project team progress and feedback. (This includes learning cycle update meetings and integration events.)
7. Follow through with frequent gemba walks, including leadership whenever possible.

To start the journey on solid ground, a leader should look for evidence that the teams are using the innovative lean development practices, behaviors, and habits, and encourage them to continue with what is there and build to complete the picture. The idea is to "catch" the team members doing something right and coach them to repeat, expand, and improve as they move forward. Leaders must be positive about what they find and reinforce the principles of innovative lean development until the cultural change is permanent.

We encourage you to get started. Start small and show some success. Then, grow your success organically from one team to the next. Engage all levels of leadership in the journey, and always learn, adjust, and keep going. The results, as they come, will speak for themselves and promote the process.

Appendix A:
Learning Cycle Planning Guide

Plan

- Review project charter with leadership
- Define the gaps—or the learning objectives to close
- Confirm commitment to the plan
- Scope the learning cycle with objectives and questions
- Prioritize the objectives into this and later learning cycles
- Update the block plan
- Pull in key project activities from milestones and tollgates
- Fill out the learning cycle scope document for the next (or first) learning cycle

Design

- Define the problem and learning objectives to be solved. These objectives define the gap between what you want and what you don't have. Innovation is used to fill the gap.
- Label and define the key customer values, and if the values are not completely known do additional research with the user of your proposed innovation whether it is a product, process, or service.
- Further define the gap between customer needs and current solutions.
- Create a baseline using existing solutions, both your own and those of your competitors, that attempt to fill that gap currently.

- Define set-based concepts.
- Develop a concept selection vehicle (concept selection matrix).
- State your learning objectives.
- Generate as many ideas as possible for filling the gap.
- List questions to answer (what, how, when, where).
- Tie these questions to tasks to be done by team members.
- Drive task completion with an accountability board.

Build

- Prototype
- Drive task completion with an accountability board

Test

- Evaluate the prototypes
- Validate with the customer
- Validate your ideas for filling the gap with a customer group or with trusted representatives of the customer group.
- Evaluate test results
- Drive task completion with an accountability board

Review

- Review prototypes across the team and with management
- Evaluate concepts; narrow if appropriate
- Document the knowledge gained
- Identify remaining gaps to be filled; these feed the next cycle
- Manage and resolve flow interruptions

Appendix B:
Knowledge Capture A3
Template and Instructions

Product Knowledge Database	A3		Author	name	Location	division, city	Keywords for searching:
			E-mail	e-mail address	Phone	number	keyword1, keyword2, keyword3, keyword4

Issue or Problem stated as a question

problem statement here

Trade-off curves, visual models, charts, graphs

text, pictures, diagrams, or graphs to visualize the knowledge

Historical background:

Historical background:

Countermeasures (business, legal) or other guidelines

text on how we can live within the design space or alter the design parameters

Root cause analysis

Root cause analysis text here

References, experts, or other data sources

add references and data sources

Lean Product Development   *A3 Knowledge Capture*

Knowledge and key takeaways

- An A3 report presents the essential information about one focused subject on a single large sheet of paper, using visual models to deepen shared understanding.
- The A3 is a record of knowledge discussed by a team during the development period.
- An A3 can be used for retrieval of historical information.
- An open shared database such as Sharepoint or Wikipedia can be used to store and catalog A3 sheets.

Keywords

- Toyota and other companies have used knowledge capture sheets in paper form for many years.
- However, keywords can be added to the spreadsheet for later reference from an online system such as Sharepoint or a Wiki style search engine. In order for online, open-text searches to work with the keywords, they must be added as attributes of the document.

Common elements—in a versatile format

- Write a brief (but complete) statement of the current problem or issue
- Background of the problem (research)
- A root cause analysis of the problem being solved, with references used
- Visual representations of the options or solutions
- Other information needed for the author to communicate a complete picture of the piece of knowledge being documented

Root cause analysis

This often takes the form of a causal diagram, a format invented by Dr. Allen Ward for engineers. This is also known as a fish-bone problem diagram. Other types of root cause analysis also work.

Excel format

- Each white area is a merged cell with text wrap turned on. This cell can be split into a text area and a picture area with the Format option.

Countermeasures (business, legal) or other guidelines

Countermeasures include design alterations needed to fit within the design parameters. Some examples might be material selection for sustainable green product design, legal concerns, feature changes, design tolerance changes, etc.

References, experts, or other data sources

This is an area to capture the sources of information used to solve the problem. They might include books, articles, web sites, or the names of experts consulted during the problem solving process.

Bibliography

Graupp, Patrick and Wrona, Robert J. *The TWI Workbook*. New York: Productivity Press, 2006.

Huthwaite, Bart. *Lean Design Solutions*. Mackinac Island, MI: Institute for Lean Innovation, 2004.

Huthwaite, Bart. *The Rules of Innovation*. Mackinac Island, MI: Institute for Lean Innovation, 2004.

Kelley, Tom. *The Art of Innovation*. New York: Doubleday, 2001.

Kelley, Tom. *The Ten Faces of Innovation*. New York: Doubleday, 2005.

Mann, David. *Creating a Lean Culture*. New York: Productivity Press, 2005.

Morgan, James M. and Liker, Jeffery K. *The Toyota Product Development System*. New York: Productivity Press, 2006.

NCMS Study, "Product Development Process—Methodology & Performance Measures Final Report," January 31, 2000. http://products.ncms.org/reports.htm.

Rattenbury, John. *A Living Architecture*. Rohnert Park, CA and Fullbridge, UK: Pomegranate, 2000.

Robinson, Alan G. and Schroeder, Dean M. *Ideas Are Free*. San Francisco, CA: Berret-Koehler Publishers, 2004.

Rubinstein, Moshe F. and Firstenberg, Iris R. *The Minding Organization: Bring the Future to the Present and Turn Creative Ideas into Business Solutions*. New York: John Wiley and Sons, 1999.

Schipper, Timothy and Schmidt, Ryan. "Lean Methods for Creative Development: How to Rapidly Deliver Solutions and Capture Knowledge by Using Lean Techniques." *AME Target Magazine*, August 2006.

Ward, Al. *Lean Product and Process Development, by Al Ward*. Cambridge, MA: Lean Enterprise Institute, 2007.

Womack, James P. and Jones, Daniel T. *Lean Thinking: Banish Waste and Create Wealth in Your Corporation*. New York: Simon & Schuster, 1996.

Womack, James P., Jones, Daniel T., and Roos, Daniel. *The Machine That Changed the World: The Story of Lean Production*. New York: HarperPerennial, 1991.

Bibliography

Glossary

A3—A single-page document containing information to share, such as knowledge captured or a process improvement plan. The A3 gets its name from the metric-size sheet of paper, roughly equivalent to 11 × 17 inches.

Accountability board or daily accountability board—A visual system used for tracking individual tasks that support the team or group objectives.

Agile resource model—The practice of quickly and temporarily shifting resources among different parts of an organization in response to the need for additional effort to complete a project on time.

Block plan—A high-level project plan listing the learning cycles that need to be accomplished before moving on to the implementation phase.

Concept selection matrix—A tool used to capture and compare the ideas from set-based design within the framework of a learning cycle.

Continuous improvement—The capstone in any lean architecture is to strive for perfection and to seek to better the process or product through incremental, small improvements resulting in higher quality and less waste.

Controlled release of work—The technique of limiting the amount of work entering a process so that the process is not overburdened and the work that is already in process can be completed.

Cycle time through a process (C/T)—The elapsed time for a unit of work to move through a process step, including the process time.

Deductive thinking—A method of thinking for moving logically, or in an orderly way, toward a solution.

Development council—A board of decision makers, representing all the key disciplines, who meet frequently, decide jointly, and respond quickly to problems and flow interrupters.

Flawless execution—A description of a project that moves through the implementation phase with minimal or no rework.

Flow interrupters—Anything that interrupts the flow of development or causes delays in the completion of the learning cycles.

Flow or continuous flow—The movement through a set of process steps without interruption and no inventory buildup between the process steps.

Gemba walk—The act of visiting the place where a process occurs in order to view the work as it is being done and to talk with the people doing the work; provides a snapshot of the process at a point in time for the purpose of identifying problems and opportunities for improvement. Gemba is a Japanese term meaning "the actual place."

Heuristic—The process of discovery or finding a solution when the path and process to deliver the solution is not predetermined or known.

Inductive thinking—A method of thinking starting with the end-in-view and working backwards to find the answer.

Integration event—The conclusion of single or multiple learning cycles accomplished either in sequence or in parallel, finishing in a single milestone event, involving the building of a prototype based on the learning from all of the learning cycles.

IT—Information technology.

Kaizen—A Japanese word translated to mean a process improvement activity. Kaizen comes from two root words, loosely translated as Kai for change, and Zen for good.

Knowledge capture—The act of capturing the knowledge gained in development at the point in time when the knowledge is first discovered.

Knowledge gaps—The gaps between the desired solution and what is currently known.

Knowledge management—An open site used to capture, categorize, index, and share knowledge gained from various initiatives.

Leader standard work—A document describing the leader's repeated and periodic activities to examine the lean system and the activities of the people in the lean system.

Lean—Combining operational excellence with value-based strategies to produce steady growth and continuous improvement.

Lean culture—An idea that is created in the mind, as an inference, consisting of the collective behaviors, practices, and habits of a community of people implementing a lean system.

Lean visual controls—A visual (or electronic) means of monitoring a process to expose problems.

Learning cycle—Short, focused development bursts, usually 2 to 4 weeks in duration.

Learning cycle objectives—See objectives.

Learning cycle scope document—The governing document for the learning cycles; lists the objectives required to move toward the discoveries needed to achieve the solution, the key questions to answer for each objective, and the high-level tasks that need to be accomplished to answer the questions.

MBDC—McDonough Braungart Design Chemistry, the consultancy that created Cradle to Cradle Design, a strategy to realize sustainable product development.

Objectives—The learning cycle objectives are the high-level problem statements that describe the learning that needs to be accomplished within the current learning cycle.

Pace—The time it takes to complete repeated tasks.

Percent complete and accurate (%C&A)—The measure of the first-pass yield, or an estimate of the quality of the work as it is received.

Phase gate process—See waterfall process.

Pitch—The frequency of checking work; always a multiple of pace.

Plan-do-check-act (PDCA)—A process improvement activity (a.k.a. kaizen effort); a 4-step process involving (1) planning, (2) taking immediate action (doing) to improve a system, (3) checking the results, and (4) acting on the things learned from completing the first three actions.

Predictive measures—Measurements of early concepts that are done very early in the development process to learn whether or not the solutions envisioned are viable.

Process measures—Measures of the customer's experience when interacting with a company or organization across a value stream, reflecting the experiences across functional boundaries in the organization.

Process time (P/T)—The time spent doing value-added work.

Prototyping—A way to reduce risks in the development process by building and quickly testing ideas and answering learning cycle questions through the construction of models and experiments.

Queue time or wait time (W/T)—The amount of time that work sits in a queue or inbox before it enters the next process step.

Rapid prototyping—Prototyping done on a very short timetable to test solutions within a learning cycle framework.

Set-based design—Carrying multiple unproven concepts forward in parallel, in contrast to taking a single "point-based" solution forward through the development process.

Standard work—The procedures and steps created to maintain a lean system at the team or individual level.

Swarming resource model—See agile resource model.

Systemic issues—Problems that occur in a supporting process during development that touch the value stream every time; highlighted as potential targets for improvement in the value stream.

Takt or takt time—A short, repeated unit of time that defines the pace of a process.

Total cycle time—Cycle time + wait time = total cycle time, which is the time it takes to complete all of the activities in an entire value stream, including all cycle times and wait times.

Toyota paradox—Spending more time on early concepts by carrying multiple concepts forward, which reduces overall project time because of less rework later in the process.

Trade-off curve—A graphical representation of opposing variables used to optimize a design.

Transactional process—A noniterative, repeatable value stream.

Unified theory of innovation—A mental framework for assembling techniques and tools in a process that enables a person to innovate.

Value stream mapping—A map drawn to focus on the process, describing process steps, data about the process steps, and information flows between process steps.

Visual boards—See accountability boards.

Visual controls—See accountability boards.

Waste—Non-value-added activity in a process.

Waste (elimination of)—The lean activity to remove or reduce the commonly found wastes within a system or process.

Waterfall process—The requirement that each phase of the project be completed and approved before the next phase can start, similar to the way each level in a series of waterfalls must fill before spilling into the next level.

Wiki—An online location for information storage, hosting information and knowledge entries written by the people who created the knowledge, but allowing peer-to-peer editing as necessary to ensure information accuracy.

Yokoten—A Japanese word defining the horizontal transfer of information and knowledge across an organization.

Index

Authors

Timothy Schipper is a graduate of Calvin College (Bachelor of Science in Mechanical Engineering) and the University of Michigan (Masters of Science). He also holds a Certification in Lean Manufacturing from the University of Michigan. He has been a tool designer, engineering educator, CAD specialist and trainer, senior product engineer, IT manager, and, most recently a lean expert and internal consultant for Steelcase, Inc., in Grand Rapids, Michigan.

He is the coauthor of *Lean Methods for Creative Development: How to Rapidly Deliver Solutions and Capture Knowledge by Using Lean Techniques* (AME Target, August 2006), which sparked the interest of others outside his company in the methods used to systematically innovate and implement lean development methods. He has presented the concepts found in *Innovative Lean Development: How to Create, Implement and Maintain a Learning Culture Using Fast Learning Cycles* at conferences, and he has facilitated workshops with numerous teams who have applied these concepts to product and information technology development. He has also facilitated many lean workshops for process improvement at Steelcase, Inc. He has worked on lean projects in manufacturing, but has specialized in lean applications in the office. All of these experiences led to the material and concepts in this book.

Tim lives in Grand Rapids, Michigan, with his wife, Karen, and their three children, Laura, Anna, and Peter, where they enjoy many outdoor activities together. He is active in civic and church organizations in his community.

Contact information: schipper.timothy@gmail.com.

Mark Swets has facilitated more than 30 lean workshops at Steelcase, Inc., in Grand Rapids, Michigan. He has led teams who have applied lean development techniques in product development, information technology application development, sales strategy development, and business model development.

Mark is a graduate of the University of Michigan, earning both a Bachelor of Science and a Master of Science degree in mechanical engineering. His work experience includes 23 years of project and program management in product development with Steelcase, Inc., Herman Miller, Inc., Chrysler Corporation, and as an independent consultant.

Currently, Mark works for Steelcase as an office lean consultant and is a frequent speaker on lean development concepts. He lives in Grand Rapids, Michigan, with his wife, Cheri, and their two children, John and Jenna.

Contact information: swets.mark@gmail.com.